Marrakesh

DIRECTIONS

WRITTEN AND RESEARCHED BY

Daniel Jacobs

ROUGH
GUIDES

NEW YORK • LONDON • DELHI
www.roughguides.com

Contents

Introduction to

Marrakesh

Marrakesh has always had a mystique about it. A city of immense beauty – low, red and tentlike below the dramatic peaks of the High Atlas mountains – its narrow alleys beg discovery while its bustling thoroughfares infuse the visitor with the city's excitement and vitality. Arguably the last outpost of the Mediterranean before the Sahara, Marrakesh is still steeped in nomadic and West African influences. Nowhere is this fact more evident than among the crowds and performers of the Jemaa el Fna, the main square at the heart of the old town. Here you'll find a constant reminder that Marrakesh was once the entrepot for goods (gold, ivory and slaves) brought by caravan across the desert.

The last few years have seen Marrakesh well and truly established as Morocco's **capital of chic**, attracting the rich and famous from Europe and beyond. Though the vast majority of its residents are poor by any European standard, an increasing number of wealthy visitors are taking up residence and their influence on the tourist experience is evident.

◄ Spice shop

Like all Moroccan cities, Marrakesh is a **town of two halves**: the ancient

When to visit

Weatherwise, **spring** (March–May) and **autumn** (Sept–Nov) are the best times to see Marrakesh – it'll be sunny but not too hot. At the height of **summer** (June–Aug), however, daytime temperatures regularly reach a roasting 38ºC, and don't fall below a sweaty 20ºC at night. In **winter** (Dec–Feb) the temperature may reach a pleasant 18ºC by day, but it can be grey and even wet; after dark, temperatures often drop to just 4ºC. Expect **accommodation** to be much in demand at Easter and at Christmas, when you should book well ahead.

walled Medina, founded by Sultan Youssef Ben Tachfine back in the Middle Ages, and the colonial Ville Nouvelle, built by the French in the mid-twentieth century. Each has its own delights – the Medina with its ancient palaces and mansions, its labyrinthine souks and its deeply traditional way of life; and the Ville Nouvelle with its pavement cafés, its trendy

▲ Riyad Al Moussika

boutiques and its gardens and boulevards.

Marrakesh is a memorable place to visit, and it can catch you with its magic at odd moments – perhaps while you're strolling across the Jemaa el Fna at night, amid the smoky plumes and delicious aromas rising from the foodstalls, or maybe while sitting in a garden full of fountains under the matchless minaret of the Koutoubia Mosque, or even when you're browsing in the smart boutiques of the new town or the bustling souks of the old. The city's charms are endless and you'll find delightful sights, tastes, smells and experiences in all of its corners.

It won't take you long to see why Marrakesh is called the **Red City**. The natural red ochre pigment that bedecks its walls and buildings can at times seem dominant, but there's no shortage of other colours, and few cities as vibrant as this one. Marrakesh breathes the scents of the Middle East and Africa: the spices, the incense, the fresh wood being cut and crafted in workshops right there on the street. Yet simultaneously it oozes a French-inspired elegance in its cool riads, haute cuisine, stylish boutiques and gorgeous clothes. Whatever the wider influences, Marrakesh is first and foremost a Moroccan

▼ Ben Youssef Medersa

▲ Koutobia Minaret at night

city – *the* Moroccan city, even – basking in Morocco's unique combination of Arab and Berber culture, that infuses its architecture, its craftwork, its cooking, and its people.

For visitors, the **Jemaa el Fna** is undoubtedly the focus, a place without parallel in the world; really no more than an open space, it's also the stage for a long-established ritual in which shifting circles of onlookers gather round groups of acrobats, musicians, dancers, storytellers, comedians and fairground acts. It is always compelling, no matter how many times you return.

Almost as intriguing are the city's **architectural attractions**: the delicate Granada-style carving of the Saadian Tombs; the magnificent rambling ruin of the El Badi Palace; the stately interior of the Bahia Palace; the exquisite Ben Youssef Medersa, a beautifully decorated

Koranic school; and, above all, the Koutoubia Minaret, the most perfect Islamic monument in North Africa, whose shape and lightness of feel set the standard for all the minarets of Morocco.

Aside from these must-sees, however, the **Medina** is the city's prime attraction; losing yourself amid this maze of irregular streets and alleys is one of the great pleasures of a visit to Marrakesh. Within its twelfth-century walls you'll find a profusion of mosques, Koranic

▲ Berber dancers

schools and *zaouias* (tombs of holy men and women), amid what is, for most Western visitors, an exotic **street life**, replete with itinerant knife-grinders and fruit sellers, mules bearing heavy goods through the narrow thoroughfares, and country people in town to sell wares spread out upon the ground. It's also within the Medina that you'll find the city's main **museums**: the Marrakesh Museum, housed in a beautiful nineteenth-century palace; Dar Si Said, with its amaz-

▼ Medina Souk

ing collection of woodwork artefacts; and the Maison Tiskiwin, with exhibits on the trans-Saharan connection between Marrakesh and Timbuktu.

In the Medina's many traditional workplaces, **artisans** such as blacksmiths, weavers, hatters, tanners and carpenters still ply ancient trades. Many of their wares end up in the Medina's **souks**, where you can spend hours wandering labyrinthine passages in search of souvenirs and haggling for handicrafts over endless cups of mint tea. Marrakesh's modern shops may lack the quaint charm of the souks, but they're worth perusing for low-priced

▲ Tagine, Chez Bahia restaurant

leatherware, household accessories and fine *objets d'art*.

For **dining**, as much as for shopping, Marrakesh is a city of new experiences. You can feast on classic Moroccan dishes like pastilla (sweet poultry pie) and tanjia (jugged beef or lamb) in the palatial splendour of an eighteenth-century Medina mansion, or enjoy delicious tajine (Moroccan casserole) or couscous at any of the Jemaa el Fna's night-time food stalls. The city also has its share of fine French and Italian restaurants, and boasts a surprisingly exuberant nightlife.

When you need a break from the bustle of the city streets, you'll find beautiful, historic and unexpectedly extensive **gardens** all around the city. Also within a couple of hours' striking distance are the peaks and valleys of the High Atlas **mountains**, where wild flowers dot pastoral landscapes beneath the rugged wildness of sheer rock and snow. Finally, just three hours away on the **coast**, is the friendly, picturesque walled town of Essaouira. It's a centre for fine art as much as water sports, not to mention some excellent seafood dining.

▼ Essaouira

Marrakesh
AT A GLANCE

THE JEMAA EL FNA

All of Moroccan life is here in this magical square – traditional performers, fortune-tellers, hawkers and ordinary Moroccans seduced by the unique vibe.

THE SOUTHERN MEDINA

Less crowded than the Northern Medina, the area south of the Jemaa el Fna is the more stately and relaxed part of the walled city.

The Jemaa el Fna ▶

▼ El Badi Palace

▲ Tomb of Sidi Abdel Aziz

THE NORTHERN MEDINA

The section of the walled city north of the Jemaa el Fna is home to Marrakesh's souks and most of the artisans' workshops. This is the liveliest and most bustling part of town.

THE VILLE NOUVELLE

Founded by the French when they took over in 1912, the new city outside the Medina walls is the centre of Marrakesh's nightlife and café culture, and the location of its poshest restaurants and chic boutiques.

▲ Dining at Pacha

THE GARDENS AND THE PALMERY

Marrakesh is surrounded by green, with a trio of classic gardens: the huge, walled Agdal, the Menara with its olive and citrus groves, and the exquisitely designed Majorelle. Northeast of town is the palmery, a rambling oasis of date trees.

▼ Menara Gardens

Ideas

The big six

As a visitor to Marrakesh, you won't find any shortage of things to see and do – almost every nook and cranny of the Medina has something of interest, and even shopping and eating out can provide a whole new cultural experience. Among the sights, the must-sees include two impressive palaces (one in ruins, the other restored), the most ornate burial site in North Africa, a beautifully designed 1920s garden, and the most amazing city square in the whole world.

▲ **Bahia Palace**

The ideal of Arabic domestic architecture expressed in a classic nineteenth-century palace.

P.64 ▸ THE SOUTHERN MEDINA

▲ **Koutoubia Mosque**

The classic Moroccan minaret, simply perfect in its proportions and its decoration.

P.53 ▸ JEMAA EL FNA AND THE KOUTOUBIA

◀ El Badi Palace

The "incomparable Palace", now an incomparable ruin.

P.61 ▸ THE SOUTHERN MEDINA AND AGDAL GARDENS

▼ Saadian Tombs

The most exquisitely decorated mausoleum in North Africa, encrusted in fine tilework and dripping with carved stucco stalactites.

P.61 ▸ THE SOUTHERN MEDINA

▲ The Jemaa el Fna

A city square that's an open-air circus, starring snake charmers, acrobats, story-tellers and musicians.

P.81 ▸ JEMAA EL FNA AND THE KOUTOUBIA

▼ Majorelle Garden

A brilliant designer garden, with cacti, bamboo groves, lily ponds and a stunning, cobalt-blue Art Deco pavilion.

P.86 ▸ THE VILLE NOUVELLE AND PALMERY

Marrakesh motifs

The features and motifs of Moroccan architecture are pretty much standard, but each theme has produced myriad variations. Islam's suspicion of representational art – making an image of a person or an animal is considered but a short step from idolatry – has given rise to a penchant for geometrical designs. In Marrakesh's palaces you'll find rich stuccowork, painted wooden ceilings and stained-glass windows. Religious buildings are especially likely to be decorated with *zellij* (mosaic tilework), particularly around the *mihrab* (niche indicating the direction of Mecca); motifs like *darj w ktarf* (cheek and shoulder) or *shabka* (net) usually adorn the minaret.

▲ Painted wooden ceilings

The cedarwood ceilings of Marrakesh's mansions and palaces are adorned with beautiful hand-painted traditional designs; some of the best can be seen at the Bahia Palace.

P.60 ▸ THE SOUTHERN MEDINA AND AGDAL GARDENS

▼ Zellij

Every building with zellij tilework actually uses its own motif, based on a star with a specific number of points.

P.60 ▸ THE SOUTHERN MEDINA AND AGDAL GARDENS

▶ Stucco & Carved cedarwood

Especially in the form of panels and lintels, cedarwood carved with inscriptions and stylistic designs surmounts walls, doorways and recessed fountains. This is often paired with stucco as some of the most intricate designs are carved into plaster on lintels, cornices and walls. This example is in the Ben Youssef Medersa.

P.61 & 76 ▶ THE NORTHERN MEDINA

▼ Castellations

The battlements atop so many of Marrakesh's gates and palaces are decorative as much as defensive.

P.70 ▶ THE NORTHERN MEDINA

▼ Darj w ktarf

This fleur de lys-like pattern, here used above the windows at the top of the Koutoubia, has been a favourite in Moroccan architecture since the time of the Almohads.

P.51 ▶ THE JEMAA EL FNA AND THE KOUTOUBIA

Souvenirs

There are plenty of wonderful souvenirs to buy in Marrakesh – among them rugs and carpets, pottery and ceramics, silver jewellery, inlaid wood (marquetry) and leather. Whatever you buy, and wherever you buy it, you're expected to bargain. There are no hard and fast rules to bargaining – it is really about paying what something is worth to you. Don't think that you need to pay a specific fraction of the first asking price: some sellers start near their lowest price, while others will make a deal for as little as a tenth of the initial price.

▲ Tyre crafts

Used car and bicycle tyres are turned into kitsch but appealing picture frames and mirror frames, as well as more practical buckets and baskets.

P.60 ▶ THE SOUTHERN MEDINA AND AGDAL GARDENS

▼ Thuya marquetry

Some lovely items are made from the wood and root of the thuya tree, often inlaid with other woods.

P.70 ▶ THE NORTHERN MEDINA

▶ Carpets

Handmade rugs and klims from all over southern Morocco can be found in Marrakesh stores, where they are displayed, compared and haggled for over a cup of mint tea.

P.70 ▸ THE NORTHERN MEDINA

◀ Musical instruments

Lutes, whether classic, wooden ouds or rustic, skin-covered ginbris, as well as drums made of wood or glazed earthenware, make good souvenirs and fine instruments if you can play them.

P.80 ▸ THE SOUTHERN MEDINA

▼ Ceramics

Fine pottery from the kilns at Salé and Sati on the coast is on sale at most of Marrakesh's souvenir outlets, even in the municipal market.

P.86 ▸ THE VILLE NOUVELLE AND PALMERY

▼ Teapots

The perfect vessel for making "le whisky marocain" (as mint tea is jokingly known) – though the right sort of mint might be hard to find once you're home.

P.51 ▸ THE JEMAA EL FNA AND THE KOUTOUBIA

Houses of prayer

Religion has always dominated life here, and the mosque lies at the very heart of the community. As well as the *jemaa*, a mosque designed for communal Friday prayers, there is the *masjid*, an everyday neighbourhood mosque, and the *zaouia*, the tomb of a holy person, whose blessing is believed to touch those who pray within. Attached to many mosques is a *medersa*, or religious school; *medersas* were at one time the only source of formal education. The city also has its synagogues, catering for a Jewish community no less religious than their Muslim neighbours, and of course a Catholic church, built by French colonialists in commemoration of Christian martyrs who died here.

▲ Almoravid Koubba

This small domed structure is the only piece of Almoravid-era architecture left standing in Morocco, and was probably used for performing ablutions before prayer.

P.74 ▸ THE NORTHERN MEDINA

▲ Ben Youssef Medersa

Carved wood, stucco and tilework – no surface is left undecorated in this ancient former Koranic school

P.76 ▸ THE NORTHERN MEDINA

▲ Lazama Synagogue

This kabbalistic chart, in the Jewish quarter's most important synagogue, underlines the importance of mysticism in local religion.

P.65 ▸ THE SOUTHERN MEDINA

▶ Église des Saints-Martyrs

The pretty little Catholic church, hidden away down a quiet backstreet in the Ville Nouvelle.

P.88 ▸ THE VILLE NOUVELLE AND PALMERY

▼ Zaouia of Sidi Bel Abbes

The tomb of Marrakesh's most important holy man, patron saint of the city's blind.

P.79 ▸ THE NORTHERN MEDINA

Dining

With some sumptuous dining to be had in Marrakesh, gourmets won't go hungry. The mainstay of Moroccan cuisine is the tajine, a casserole traditionally cooked on its own charcoal stove called a *kanoun*. Many of the best places to eat are palace restaurants, housed in beautifully restored old mansions (though choose carefully: the worst of these are real tourist traps, with mediocre food and inflated prices). Most restaurants offer a set menu of starter, main course and dessert, sometimes with tea and coffee thrown in and, at grander establishments, additional courses and even entertainment.

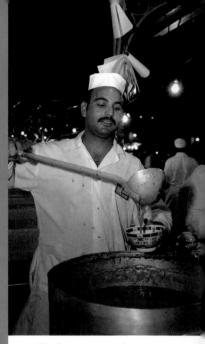

▲ Harira soup

A thick, hearty broth sold in the Jemaa, on the street, and at almost any restaurant in town; like every Moroccan town, Marrakesh has its own way of making it.

P.51 ▶ THE JEMAA EL FNA AND THE KOUTOUBIA

▼ Tajine

The classic tajines are chicken with olive and preserved lemon, and lamb with prunes and almonds.

P.81 ▶ THE JEMAA EL FNA AND THE KOUTOUBIA

◀ Couscous

Berber in origin, this is the classic north African dish: steamed semolina pellets, moist and aromatic. It's served with meat, fish or vegetables – classically seven vegetables in fact. Try it at Le Tobsil.

P.51 ▶ THE JEMAA EL FNA AND THE KOUTOUBIA

▶ Tanjia

The dish for which Marrakesh is known in the rest of Morocco – succulent, tender jugged meat, cooked in the embers of the fire that heats the local hammam.

P.51 ▶ THE JEMAA EL FNA AND THE KOUTOUBIA

▼ Pastilla

Where better to try this rich, sweet poultry pie than at Al Fassia, which specializes in the cuisine of Fes, where pastilla originates.

P.93 ▶ THE VILLE NOUVELLE AND PALMERY

▼ Snail stew

You pull the molluscs – bought from vendors in the Jemaa el Fna – out of their shells with a tooth-pick, then drink the soup.

P.51 ▶ THE JEMAA EL FNA AND THE KOUTOUBIA

Dead Marrakesh

This is a city that respects its dead. Muslims are never cremated after death, but are buried with their heads towards Mecca. Elaborate gravestones are not the custom, though somebody particularly holy may have a domed tomb – a koubba – erected over their grave. Some two hundred such holy men and women, known as marabouts, are buried in Marrakesh; the tombs of the seven most prominent (the "seven saints") have formed a circuit for pilgrims since the seventeenth century.

▲ **Tomb of Sidi Abdel Aziz**

This *zaouia* is among the smallest of the tombs of the city's seven saints.

P.76 ▶ THE NORTHERN MEDINA

▶ Miâara Jewish cemetery

Hump-like graves standing in neat rows as far as the eye can see characterize this seventeenth-century plot, serving Marrakesh's once sizeable Jewish community.

P.65 ▶ THE SOUTHERN MEDINA

◀ Saadian Tombs

The mausoleum for a whole dynasty of sultans, from the great Ahmed el Mansour to the mad Moulay Yazid.

P.61 ▶ THE SOUTHERN MEDINA

▼ Tomb of Fatima Zohra

A whitewashed shrine in the shadow of the Koutoubia, and commemorating one of Marrakesh's few female saints.

P.54 ▶ THE JEMAA EL FNA AND THE KOUTOUBIA

▼ The European cemetery

Marrakesh's most atmospheric burial ground, with war graves and grand colonial tombs.

P.89 ▶ THE VILLE NOUVELLE AND PALMERY

Style and attire

You probably wouldn't want to walk down the streets of Liverpool or Los Angeles wearing a traditional Moroccan robe, but you might want to lounge around at home in one. Moroccan slippers are a favourite buy – exotic, stylish and comfortable. For women, accessories such as scarves and chunky, exotic jewellery are worth considering, as are the dresses on sale at the city's boutiques, not to mention exquisite Morocco leather in the form of clothes, bags and belts.

▲ Jewellery

Arabic jewellery can sometimes be a little too gaudy for Western tastes, but some of the smaller, more modest pieces – including silver bangles and chunky rings – can add a touch of exotic Moroccan style once you're back home.

P.51 ▸ THE JEMAA EL FNA AND THE KOUTOUBIA

▼ Jellabas

Popular with hippy visitors in the 1960s, the *jellaba* is ordinary streetwear here, but works better as a nightgown in the West.

P.70 ▸ THE NORTHERN MEDINA

▲ Scarves

The kissaria, at the heart of the souk area, is the place to find silk and cotton scarves in any colour you could imagine.

P.70 ▶ THE NORTHERN MEDINA

▼ Leather

Moroccan leather is famously soft and sumptuous, and comes in a myriad of forms from belts, bags and clothing at the posh boutiques in the Ville Nouvelle, to pouffes and even book covers in the souk.

P.86 ▶ THE VILLE NOUVELLE AND PALMERY

▲ Knitted caps

Brightly coloured skullcaps – you'll need short hair to wear them – are a big favourite with Moroccan men.

P.70 ▶ THE NORTHERN MEDINA

▼ Babouches

Moroccan leather slippers, traditionally yellow, but available in plenty of other colours and fabrics and in varying states of decoration.

P.70 ▶ THE NORTHERN MEDINA

Museums and galleries

Marrakesh's museums are arguably of interest more for the buildings that house them than for the exhibits they contain, but you'll certainly want to look around inside if you have a special interest in woodcarving or in Moroccan and Islamic arts. Lately a new wave of modern artists have created a stir in Marrakesh, and a handful of exciting art galleries have sprung up to exhibit their work, both in the Medina and in the Ville Nouvelle.

▲ Dar Si Said

A beautiful old mansion with a great collection of carved cedarwood, some of it adorning the building itself, not to mention some wonderful stuccowork.

P.60 ▸ THE SOUTHERN MEDINA AND AGDAL GARDENS

▼ Maison Tiskiwin

A unique collection of Moroccan and Malian artefacts illustrating the trans-Saharan caravan trade with Timbuktu, on which Marrakesh's economy was once based.

P.60 ▸ THE SOUTHERN MEDINA

▲ La Galerie Bleue

The Ville Nouvelle's newest modern art gallery, exhibiting the work of Morocco's leading artists.

P.91 ▸ THE VILLE NOUVELLE AND PALMERY

▼ Islamic Arts Museum

Yves Saint Laurent's personal collection of North African carpets, ceramics and furniture, housed in a brilliant cobalt blue house amid cacti and lily ponds.

P.87 ▸ THE VILLE NOUVELLE AND PALMERY

▲ Marrakesh Museum

This imposing nineteenth-century politician's mansion now houses exhibitions of Moroccan art and sculpture.

P.74 ▸ THE NORTHERN MEDINA

Indulgent Marrakesh

There are plenty of sensual pleasures to explore in Marrakesh, often for very little money. A steam bath at a hammam comes complete, if you want it, with a massage and rub-down. Alternatively, let yourself be transported around town in a horse-drawn carriage, have a henna tattoo or order sumptuous pastries at one of the city's patisseries. For those who can afford it, the city's luxury hotels offer gourmet food, opulent furnishings and staff at your beck and call day and night.

▲ Henna tattoos

Have a semi-permanent design painted on your hands, as Moroccan women do for their wedding. It should not wash off for at least three weeks.

P.51 ▶ THE JEMAA EL FNA AND
THE KOUTOUBIA

▼ Calèche rides

Sit back in a horse-drawn carriage and ride in style around town or through the palmery.

P.132 ▶ ESSENTIALS

► La Maison Arabe

The most deluxe hotel in town boats palatial splendour in an intimate, exclusive environment. It features immaculately kept patios, superb food and even its own cookery school.

P.120 ► ACCOMMODATION

29

◄ Ice-cream at Oliveri

Marrakesh's swankiest ice-cream parlour is the place to relax over a scoop of the country's most divine frozen confections.

P.93 ► PLACES

▼ Pastries and confections

To indulge your sweet tooth, Marrakesh boasts not only French-style patisseries, but also traditional stalls in the souks offering syrup-soaked delicacies.

P.70 ► THE NORTHERN MEDINA

▼ The hammam

Men and women have separate entrances to the Turkish-style steam bath, where the principle is to sweat it all out and have all the dirt rubbed and scrubbed off. You'll emerge glowing.

P.129 ► ESSENTIALS

The city gates

Marrakesh's ramparts, 15km in circumference and 2m thick, are punctuated by nineteen city gates. Many of these are modern, though the walls themselves, made of *pisé* (clay and chalk), mostly date back to the city's foundation under the Almoravids in the eleventh century. Some of the gates are clearly defensive but others were designed to impress visitors entering. The more recent gates are much simpler – sometimes just breaches in the wall – and were added to improve access to the Medina.

▲ Bab Debbagh

The gate leading into the tanners' quarter has a complicated chicane within to obstruct any invading forces trying to enter the city.

P.78 ▶ THE NORTHERN MEDINA

▲ Bab Agnaou

This nineteenth-century gate was once the city's main entrance for common people.

P.64 ▶ THE SOUTHERN MEDINA

▲ Bab el Khemis

The "Thursday Gate" is named for the Thursday market held outside – though these days there's a market every day.

P.79 ▸ THE NORTHERN MEDINA

▼ Bab Nkob

The main gateway from the Medina to the Ville Nouvelle, and by far the busiest entrance into the walled city.

P.60 ▸ THE SOUTHERN MEDINA

▲ Bab Taghzout

Close to one of the city's important *zaouias*, this ochre gateway was part of the city walls until they were extended northward in the eighteenth century.

P.79 ▸ THE NORTHERN MEDINA

Celebrity Marrakesh

Marrakesh has been a holiday destination for the rich and famous since the 1920s. This exotic escape has gained appeal in recent years with the appearance of so many charming, beautiful and secluded deluxe riads peppering the Medina. Add in some spectacular shops and a few renowned chefs, and Marrakesh can barely keep the A-list celebs away. Movie actors, pop stars and glitterati from the world of fashion seem to love the place, and there are of course certain exclusive locales they tend to frequent.

▲ The Marrakesh Film Festival

Catherine Deneuve and Martin Scorsese are among the glitterati who have flocked to Marrakesh for this prestigious cinematic event, held in October.

P.137 ▸ ESSENTIALS

▲ Casa Lalla

Double Michelin-starred British chef Richard Neat presides over the culinary proceedings at his sleek new riad off the Jemaa el Fna.

P.56 ▸ THE JEMAA EL FNA AND THE KOUTOUBIA

▲ Hotel Riad Medina

Nowadays this place is quite upmarket, but as a down-at-heel 1960s hippy hostelry it attracted the likes of Jimi Hendrix, Frank Zappa, Cat Stevens and the Jefferson Airplane.

P.127 ▸ ACCOMMODATION

▶ Maison du Kaftan Marocain

Jean-Paul Gaultier and Samuel L. Jackson number among the customers for the beautiful chic creations at this unassuming clothes shop in the Medina.

P.82 ▸ THE NORTHERN MEDINA

▼ Hotel Mamounia

Winston Churchill heads the list of seriously important people who've stayed in this, the city's top hotel, where Alfred Hitchcock filmed James Stewart and Doris Day in *The Man Who Knew Too Much*. Sean Connery stayed here during the Marrakesh Film Festival.

P.117 ▸ ACCOMMODATION

Entertainment in the Jemaa

Without the Jemaa el Fna, said novelist Paul Bowles, Marrakesh would be just another Moroccan city, and certainly this square is the city's heart and soul. Here you'll find acrobats and storytellers, snake charmers and tooth-pullers. In the evening you can sit down to a full meal while a motley crew of itinerant musicians plays late into the night.

▲ Tooth-pullers

Their methods may look crude and brutal, but these practitioners offer the only tooth-ache treatment most Moroccans can afford.

P.60 ▶ THE SOUTHERN MEDINA

▼ Gnaoua musicians

Members of a Sufi brotherhood from West Africa are some of the Jemaa's most colour-ful performers, keeping up a rhythm till late into the night.

P.52 ▶ THE JEMAA EL FNA AND THE KOUTOUBIA

▲ Jemaa dining

Everything from spaghetti to sheeps' heads is on offer at the evening food stalls, where you can dine in an atmosphere unmatched by any restaurant.

P.51 ▸ THE JEMAA EL FNA AND THE KOUTOUBIA

▼ Fortune-tellers

In Marrakesh you can have your cards read by wise women under umbrellas, or get a talisman made up, as often as not using Koranic verses, though such practices aren't endorsed by orthodox Islam.

P.52 ▸ THE JEMAA EL FNA AND THE KOUTOUBIA

▲ Khendenjal

A spicy hot drink served with an equally spicy nut-based confection. The drink is supposedly an aphrodisiac – if you're with the right person, try it and see.

P.59 ▸ THE JEMAA EL FNA AND THE KOUTOUBIA

▼ Medicine men

Remedies, spells and potions, aphrodisiacs even, of origins animal, vegetable and mineral – and not a pill or a capsule in sight.

P.51 ▸ THE JEMAA EL FNA AND THE KOUTOUBIA

Cafés

When coffee first arrived in the Islamic world, many Muslim jurists argued that it should be banned as an intoxicant. However, more moderate voices prevailed, and the café became an important feature of life in many Muslim countries. In Morocco, its position was reinforced by the French colonials, who added their own style of café society. Today the cafés perform the role that bars have traditionally had in many Western countries; largely a male preserve, they provide a place to hang out with friends or watch football on TV. They're also ideal for a morning croissant, or a pot of mint tea come the afternoon.

▲ Café Le Siroua

A small, friendly café with excellent coffee; handy for breakfast and open long hours.

P.93 ▸ THE VILLE NOUVELLE AND PALMERY

▼ Bougainvillea Café

A pretty little patio in the heart of the Medina, and very handy for a coffee break while shopping in the souks.

P.83 ▸ THE NORTHERN MEDINA

► Café-Restaurant Argana

Pop up for a pot of tea and enjoy one of the best views over the Jemaa el Fna.

P.57 ► THE JEMAA
EL FNA AND
THE KOUTOUBIA

◄ Café Les Negociants

Slap-bang in the middle of the Ville Nouvelle, and just the place to watch the world go by while relaxing with a coffee and croissant.

P.92 ► THE VILLE NOUVELLE AND
PALMERY

▼ Café des Épices

Great views over the hubbub of the Rahba Kedima from the terrace of this bright little café.

P.84 ► THE NORTHERN MEDINA

▼ Café-Restaurant Toubkal

Here's a place that does tasty msammen – something between a French crepe and an Indian paratha, served with honey for breakfast.

P.56 ► THE JEMAA EL FNA AND
THE KOUTOUBIA

Green Marrakesh

Especially in summer, when temperatures rise to the high thirties Celsius (the high nineties in Fahrenheit), the middle of the day is sometimes best devoted to inactivity, and where better for that than the city's gardens. Two of them – the Agdal and Menara – were designed for that purpose. Each begins near the edge of the Medina, rambles through acres of orchards and olive groves and has, near its centre, an immense pool, once thought to cool the air. Much smaller and more tended and landscaped is the gorgeous Majorelle Garden.

▲ The Agdal gardens

Watered by ancient underground channels, the gardens were founded with the city itself and provided a picnic spot for the sultan and his entourage.

P.65 ▶ THE SOUTHERN MEDINA

▼ The palmery

Date palms and suburban villas make Marrakesh's own oasis a sought-after residential location, as well as a pleasant retreat from the city bustle.

P.89 ▶ THE VILLE NOUVELLE AND PALMERY

▶ The Menara gardens

Tranquil by day, the pool and pavilion here are the setting for a night-time "Marvels and Reflections" show of dance and acrobatics.

P.88 ▶ THE VILLE NOUVELLE AND PALMERY

▲ Majorelle Garden

Twentieth-century French painter Jacques Majorelle's beautifully landscaped garden has an impressive collection of cacti.

P.86 ▶ THE VILLE NOUVELLE AND PALMERY

▼ Bab Jedid olive grove

Olives are one of Morocco's agricultural mainstays – even in Marrakesh it's easy to find them growing. Outside Bab Jedid, you'll find them in a grove that's a popular picnic spot for Marrakshi families.

P.88 ▶ THE VILLE NOUVELLE AND PALMERY

Marrakesh nightlife

In a town where good girls don't stay out late, Marrakesh nightlife is quite restricted, but it's there if you want it. Most of the upmarket hotels have bars where a woman can at least enjoy a drink without the presumption that she must be on the game, and nightclubs where you can shake your booty to a variety of sounds. In the Medina, the Jemaa el Fna offers a very different sort of after-dark experience – open-air dining amid a veritable circus of street performers.

▲ Pacha

Marrakesh's most happening nightspot – a branch of the famous Ibiza rave club.

P.97 ▶ THE VILLE NOUVELLE AND PALMERY

▼ The Jemaa el Fna by night

Dine under the stars to the accompaniment of rhythmic Gnaoua music from the square's wandering musicians.

P.51 ▶ THE JEMAA EL FNA AND THE KOUTOUBIA

▲ Diamant Noir nightclub

North African raï sounds are the dance-floor filler at this popular downtown club.

P.97 ▸ THE VILLE NOUVELLE AND PALMERY

▼ Hotel Mamounia Casino

Top notch jacket-and-tie casino, which promises to stay open "until you run out of money".

P.69 ▸ THE SOUTHERN MEDINA

▲ Chesterfield Pub

Not as English as it would like to be, this "pub" is nonetheless one of Marrakesh's more atmospheric watering holes.

P.96 ▸ THE VILLE NOUVELLE AND PALMERY

▼ Paradise Disco

Marrakesh's poshest disco is only partially successful at being exclusive, but it's a good night out all the same.

P.98 ▸ THE VILLE NOUVELLE AND PALMERY

Artisans at work

Marrakesh is alive with cottage industries, worked by skilled artisans using methods that have barely changed over the centuries, and continuing trades that have all but died out in the West. On a wander through the Medina you'll find tanneries and smithies, weavers at their looms, hatters shaping headwear and cobblers making shoes. In many ways, these workshops are much more interesting – though no larger – than the shops selling the goods they produce. Another perk is that the artisans may sell you items you see being finished or even custom-make something just to your taste.

▲ Tanners

The dye pits look – and smell – like something out of Dante's Inferno, a result of the pigeon droppings and other unpleasant substances used to tan leather in this mucky medieval trade.

P.78 ▸ THE NORTHERN MEDINA

▼ Blacksmiths

Railings, window grilles or furniture – no metal creation is too complex for local blacksmiths and ironmongers.

P.70 ▸ THE NORTHERN MEDINA

43

▶ Dyers

The dyers have the Medina's most colourful souk, hung with hanks of wool in all the colours of the rainbow.

P.73 ▶ THE NORTHERN MEDINA

▲ Carpet weavers

Handlooms are still used to produce Moroccan carpets, each a one-off piece.

P.72 ▶ THE NORTHERN MEDINA

▼ Leatherworkers

Fresh from the city's tanneries, leather is cut, stitched and studded into all manner of consumer durables.

P.74 ▶ THE NORTHERN MEDINA

Sports and activities

Within easy reach of Marrakesh are the High Atlas mountains, perfect for a hike or, from December to April, skiing. Just a little further away, coastal Essaouira is a popular centre for windsurfing. Closer at hand there are three eighteen-hole golf courses just outside Marrakesh itself. For something more sedentary, you can take in the town from a double-decker sightseeing bus, or ride around the palmery on the back of a camel.

▲ Sightseeing tour

Hop on and off where you like – the big red double-decker will take you past all the sights in town.

P.132 ▸ ESSENTIALS

▼ Atlas trekking

Crystalline mountain air, snowy peaks and green valleys await trekkers and hikers in the High Atlas.

P.102 ▸ ATLAS EXCURSIONS

▶ Golf

Morocco's late king, Hassan II, enjoyed a spot of golf, and the country has some top-class courses, including three excellent ones around Marrakesh.

P.125 ▶ THE VILLE NOUVELLE AND PALMERY

◀ Camel riding

If you've never tried a ride on the ship of the desert, pop up to the Palmery and be Lawrence of Arabia for the afternoon.

P.86 ▶ THE VILLE NOUVELLE AND PALMERY

▼ Windsurfing

Reliable winds at Essaouira ensure some of the best windsurfing in North Africa.

P.103 ▶ ESSAOUIRA

▼ Skiing at Oukaïmeden

Just two hours from Marrakesh you'll find 20km of runs for skiers and snowboarders at all levels.

P.101 ▶ ATLAS EXCURSIONS

Marrakesh calendar

Marrakesh and its hinterland aren't short of annual events of all descriptions. Among the religious festivities are moussems, local affairs commemorating particular holy men or women. There are also sporting events and cultural festivals, notably a celebration of popular – here meaning traditional – arts.

▼ January: Marrakesh Marathon

Athletes from Morocco and abroad come to run this gruelling but scenic race around the Medina and through the palmery.

P.137 ▸ ESSENTIALS

▼ August: Moussem at Setti Fatma

You can combine a hike in the Ourika Valley with this traditional annual shindig held in commemoration of a local saint in the valley's main village.

P.101 ▸ ATLAS EXCURSIONS

▲ June: Marrakesh Popular Arts Festival

An equestrian "fantasia" is held outside the city walls every evening during this week-long festival of music, dance and folklore.

P.137 ▸ ESSENTIALS

▼ June: Gnaoua Festival

West Africa's influence on Moroccan and world music is the focus of this very special music festival held every year in Essaouira.

P.136 ▸ ESSAOUIRA

▲ September: Ramadan

Practising Muslims fast from dawn to sunset in the holy month of Ramadan; the fast is then broken each evening with a meal that traditionally features soup, dates and eggs.

P.136 ▸ ESSENTIALS

Places

Jemaa el Fna and the Koutoubia

Once upon a time, every Moroccan city had a main square where storytellers and musicians entertained the townspeople. Even then, the Jemaa el Fna drew the greatest variety of performers, and the best in every category. Today, it's the only one left. By day there are just a few entertainers, but in the evening it becomes a whole carnival; come here and you'll soon be squatting amid the onlookers and contributing a dirham or two. For a respite, the café and restaurant rooftop terraces set around it afford a view over the square and of the Koutoubia Minaret – as much a symbol of Marrakesh as Big Ben is of London.

Jemaa el Fna

Nobody is entirely sure when or how the Jemaa el Fna came into being – or even what its name means. The usual translation is "assembly of the dead", which could refer to the public display here of the heads of rebels and criminals, since the Jemaa was a place of execution well into the nineteenth century. An alternative translation is "mosque of nothing", perhaps referring to an abandoned sixteenth-century plan for a new great mosque on the site.

By day, most of the square is just a big open space, in which a handful of **snake charmers** bewitch their cobras with flutes, **medicine men** (especially in the northeast of the square) display cures and nostrums and **tooth-pullers**, wielding fearsome pliers, offer to pluck the pain from out of the heads of toothache sufferers, trays of extracted molars attesting to their skill. It isn't until late afternoon that the square really gets going. At dusk, as

in France and Spain, people come out for an early evening promenade (especially in Rue Bab Agnaou), and the square gradually fills with storytellers, acrobats and musicians (see box p.52), and the crowds who

▼ WATER SELLERS

PLACES

Jemaa el Fna and the Koutoubia

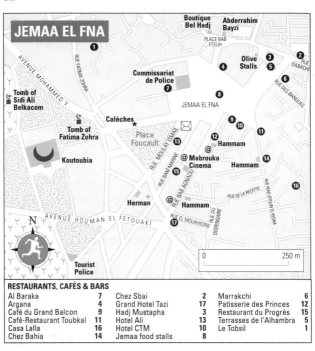

RESTAURANTS, CAFÉS & BARS

Al Baraka	7	Chez Sbai	2	Marrakchi	6
Argana	4	Grand Hotel Tazi	17	Patisserie des Princes	12
Café du Grand Balcon	9	Hadj Mustapha	3	Restaurant du Progrès	15
Café-Restaurant Toubkal	11	Hotel Ali	13	Terrasses de l'Alhambra	5
Casa Lalla	16	Hotel CTM	10	Le Tobsil	1
Chez Bahia	14	Jemaa food stalls	8		

come to see them. Most of the crowd are Moroccan of course (few foreigners, for example, will understand the storytellers' tales), but tourists also make a major contribution to both the atmosphere and the cashflow.

There are sideshow attractions too: games of hoop-the-bottle, **fortune-tellers** sitting under umbrellas with packs of fortune-telling cards at the ready and women with piping bags full of **henna** paste, ready to

Performers in the Jemaa el Fna

The tourists' favourite among the square's performers are the **snake charmers**, always photogenic, though of course you have to pay them for the privilege of a snapshot. Moroccans, however, prefer the **storytellers**, great raconteurs who draw quite a throng – it's around them that you'll see the biggest circles gathered. Also in attendance are **acrobats** and male **dancers in drag**. In the daytime, you'll see sad-looking trained **monkeys** being led around on leashes, and posing, like the cobras, for photographs, which is also nowadays the main occupation of the **tooth-pullers** and, dressed in their magnificent red regalia, the **water sellers**.

Dozens of **musicians** in the square play all kinds of instruments. In the evening there are full groups including **Gnaoua** trance-healers, members of a Sufi brotherhood of Senegalese origin, who beat out hour-long hypnotic rhythms with clanging iron castanets and pound tall drums with long curved sticks, and groups playing Moroccan popular folk music, known as *chaabi*. Late into the night, when almost everyone has gone home, you'll still find players plucking away at their lute-like *ginbris*.

paint hands, feet or arms with "tattoos" that will last up to three months (though beware of black – as opposed to natural red – henna, as this contains a toxic chemical).

For **refreshment**, stalls offer freshly squeezed orange and grapefruit juice, while neighbouring handcarts are piled high with dates, dried figs, almonds and walnuts, especially delicious in winter when they are freshly picked in the surrounding countryside.

As dusk falls, the square becomes a huge **open-air dining area**, packed with stalls lit by gas lanterns, and the air is filled with wonderful smells and plumes of cooking smoke spiralling up into the night (see box opposite).

The Koutoubia

Rising dramatically from the palm trees to the west of the square, the Koutoubia Minaret – nearly seventy metres high and visible for miles on a clear morning – is the oldest of the three great towers built by Morocco's eleventh-century Almohad rulers (the others are

the Hassan Tower in Rabat and the Giralda in Seville).

Work on the minaret probably began shortly after the Almohad conquest of the city, around 1150, and was completed under Sultan Yacoub el Mansour (ruled 1184–99).

The Koutoubia's **proportions** – a 1:5 ratio of width to height – give it an extraordinary lightness of feel and set the standard for minarets throughout Morocco. Indeed the Koutoubia displays many features that are now widespread in Moroccan architecture – the wide band of **ceramic inlay** near the top, the **castellated battlements** rising above it, the **darj w ktarf** ("cheek and shoulder" – similar to the French *fleur de lys*) – and the alternation of patterning on the different faces. At the summit are three great copper balls, thought to have been made originally of gold, possibly a gift from Yacoub el Mansour's wife, presented as penance for breaking her fast for three hours during Ramadan.

Originally the minaret was covered with plaster and painted, like the Kasbah Mosque, near

▼ KOUTOUBIA MOSQUE

the Saadian Tombs (see p.61). New floodlighting is seen to stunning effect in the evening, when the minaret and the neighbouring gardens become something of a focus for promenading Marrakshis.

The tomb of Fatima Zohra

The white *koubba* (domed mausoleum) alongside the Koutoubia is the **tomb of Fatima Zohra**, the daughter of a seventeenth-century religious leader. Tradition has it that she was a woman by day and a white dove by night; women still dedicate their children to her in the belief that her blessing will protect them.

Shops

Abderrahim Bayzi

160 Place Bab Fteuh ☎044 42 91 57. Daily 8am–8pm. Here you'll find teapots and tea glasses, lots of them, for serving up mint tea

▼ TOMB OF FATIMA ZOHRA

of course. There are aluminium pots for decoration only, and stainless steel ones that you can actually use – all in the typically Moroccan "pointed pear" shape – plus glasses both plain and fancy, many of them hand-decorated. To check prices before you start to haggle, pop round the corner to one of the hardware shops behind the Commissariat de Police in the north of the Jemaa el Fna, where you'll find similar items at fixed prices.

Boutique Bel Hadj

22 & 33 Souk Fondouk Louarzazi, Place Bab Fteuh ☎044 44 12 58. Daily 9.30am–7pm. If silver is your thing, this is the place to look, with heavy silver bracelets from around Morocco and as far afield as Afghanistan, sold by weight and purity. There's other silverware too – antique teapots for example (often as not made for the Moroccan market in Manchester), along with tea trays.

Herman

3 Rue Moulay Ismail. Daily 8am–10pm. You may be aware that the term "tajine" correctly refers, like "casserole" and "paella", not to the food but rather to the vessel in which it is cooked, a heavy ceramic plate crowned with a conical ceramic top in which the contents are steamed slowly over a low light, or more properly, over a *kanoun* (brazier) of burning charcoal. Should you wish to buy such a vessel, this unassuming little store is the place to do it. There are pretty tajines here from Fes and Safi, but the real McCoy are the heavy red earthenware jobs which hail from Sale on the coast, where the local clay is perfect for the purpose. A large-size Sale tajine will set you back

▲ SILVER JEWELLERY

40dh, and you can also buy a *kanoun* to go with it.

Olive stalls

Souk Ableuh. Daily 10am–8pm.
Located in a little square just off the Jemaa el Fna is a row of stalls with olives piled up at the front. The wrinkled black ones are the typical Moroccan olive, delicious with bread but a bit salty on their own. As for the green olives, the ones flavoured with bits of lemon are among the tastiest. Other delicacies on sale here include the spicy red harissa sauce and bright yellow lemons preserved in brine, the brine taking the edge off the lemons' acidity. Not only are these lemons a favourite ingredient in Moroccan cooking, but a jar of them also looks great on a kitchen shelf.

Cafés

Café du Grand Balcon

South side of the square, next door to the *Hotel CTM*. Daily 9am–10pm. Though not quite as close

to the action as the *Restaurant Argana* (see p.57), this place has the fullest view over the Jemaa, taking it all in from the perfect vantage point. In the evening the best tables get taken quickly, though at other times you should have no trouble getting a place with a view. It serves no food, only tea, coffee and sodas, all at relatively high prices of course.

Hotel CTM

South side of the square. Daily 7am–11pm. In addition to offering a view onto most of the square, the hotel's rooftop café does a very good-value Continental breakfast (7–11am; 20dh), but otherwise serves only drinks.

▼ HOTEL CTM

Patisseries

Patisserie des Princes

32 Rue Bab Agnaou. Daily 5am–midnight. A sparkling patisserie with mouthwatering pastries at prices that are a little high by local standards but well worth the extra. They also have treats like almond milk and ice cream. The *salon de thé* at the back is a very civilized place to take breakfast, morning coffee or afternoon tea.

Restaurants

Café-Restaurant Toubkal

Southeast corner of Jemaa el Fna, by Rue Riad Zitoun el Kedim. Daily 24hr. As well as fruit juices, home-made yoghurts and pastries, they offer a range of salads, tajines and couscous. This is also a great place for a breakfast of coffee with bread and jam or *msammen* (a paratha-like griddle bread) with honey. You'll be hard-put to spend more than 50dh.

Casa Lalla

16 Derb Jemaa ☎044 42 97 57, ⓦwww.riadcasalalla.com. 5 days a week from 8pm. If you want a gastronomic experience in Marrakesh, this is the place to come. There's no menu as such, but you're promised a parade of dishes created by master chef Richard Neat, formerly of London's *Pied à Terre*, and *Restaurant Neat* in Cannes – at both of which he earned plaudits from critics and bon viveurs, and stars from Michelin. He's now moved to Marrakesh and set up shop in this smart riad (see p.114), where you can sample his latest creations at 400dh a head excluding drinks.

Chez Bahia

50m down Rue Riad Zitoun el Kedim. Daily 6am–midnight. A café–diner offering pastilla, wonderful tajines (bubbling away at the front) and low-priced snacks, plus breakfasts of *bisara*, which is a thick pea soup with olive oil and cumin, and freshly made *harsha*, a delicious dense griddle bread with a gritty crust. You can eat well here for 50dh.

Grillade Chez Sbai

Rue Dabachi. Daily 8.30am–1am. The tables are upstairs but you order

▼ CHEZ BAHIA

downstairs at this tiny hole-in-the-wall eatery. It isn't much to look at, but the food is good, the portions are ample and the prices are low. Most customers go for the spit-roast chicken, but the best deal is a big plate of chicken shwarma with chips and salad, a snip at 22dh.

Hadj Mustapha

Souk Ableuh. Daily 8am–10pm. One of a trio of cheap hole-in-the-wall diners selling tanjia (also spelt tangia or tanzhiya), the most quintessential of Marrakshi dishes, consisting of beef, or sometimes mutton, cooked very slowly in an urn – in fact, the term tanjia actually refers to the urn. Most good restaurants in town offer tanjia, but this is where working-class Marrakshis come to eat it. If you drop by in advance, you can have it cooked to order: the meat and seasonings (garlic, cumin, nutmeg and other spices) will be placed in the urn for you and taken to the man who stokes the furnace at the local hammam. When the urn emerges from the embers a few hours later, the meat is tender and ready to eat.

Hotel Ali

Rue Moulay Ismail. Daily 6.30–10pm. This popular hotel serves a buffet supper every evening, on the roof in summer, inside during the winter. The spread features *harira*, salads, couscous and a handful of tajine-style dishes, including several vegetable ones, plus Arabic pastries and fruit for dessert. Eat as much as you like for 60dh (50dh for hotel residents).

Le Tobsil

22 Derb Abdellah Ben Hessaien ☎044 44 40 52. Daily except Tues

7.30–11pm. Sumptuous Moroccan cuisine in an intimate riad, reached by heading south down a little alley just east of Bab Laksour. This is considered by many to be the finest restaurant in town, with delicious pastilla and the most aromatic couscous you could imagine, though the wine (included in the price) doesn't match the food in quality. Worth booking ahead; the set menu – which changes daily – is 580dh.

Restaurant Al Baraka

1 Place Jemaa el Fna, by the Commissariat de Police ☎044 44 23 41, ⓦwww.albaraka.com. Daily noon–3pm & 8–11pm. A stylish Moroccan restaurant set in a beautiful garden and with a tastefully decorated interior. The food is terrific, from the range of salads (including carrot perfumed with orange blossom water) to the perfectly tender chicken and lamb tajines. In the evenings they lay on music and belly-dancing (not really Moroccan, but what the hell). Set menus 300–400dh.

Restaurant Argana

North side of the square. Daily 5am–midnight. The Jemaa's closest vantage point and not a bad place to eat either. Dishes include lamb tajine with prunes, or a seafood pastilla, a new-fangled version of the traditional poultry pie. Set menus are 90–150dh.

Restaurant Marrakchi

52 Rue des Banques ☎044 44 33 77. Daily noon–6pm & 7pm–midnight. High up above the square, the *Marrakchi* has imperial but intimate decor, impeccable service and superb food, including an indescribably

delicious pastilla. There are two set menus: the cheaper one (250dh) gives you a choice of twelve tajines or six different couscous dishes, each including a vegetarian option, or there's a 350dh menu which allows you to have a tajine *and* a couscous dish, though you'll be hard pressed to fit it all in.

Restaurant du Progrès

20 Rue Bani Marine. Daily noon–midnight. One of the best budget restaurants in town, with friendly service, huge steaming portions of couscous (go for that or the brochettes in preference to the tajines, which are rather bland), and you'll usually get change out of 50dh; if you want to be a real pig, there's a four-course set menu for 80dh.

Terrasses de l'Alhambra

Jemaa el Fna, northeast corner ☏044 42 75 70. Daily 8am–midnight. A tourist trap, yes, and the food is overpriced and not consistently good, but it does have a great location overlooking the northeastern arm of the Jemaa, with two covered terraces, menus at 115dh and 130dh and lots of pizzas, pasta and salad.

Jemaa food stalls

Marrakesh's tourist guides often suggest that the Jemaa's food stalls (open daily from dusk until 11pm) aren't very hygienic, but, as the cooking is so visible, standards of cleanliness are probably higher than in many kitchens. As well as couscous and pastilla, there are spicy **merguez** sausages, salads, fried fish and – for the more adventurous – **sheep's heads** complete with eyes.

To partake, just take a seat on one of the benches and order all you like. If you want a soft drink or mineral water with your meal, the stallholders will send a boy to get it for you. Note that stalls which don't clearly display their prices are likely to overcharge you

▼ ORANGE JUICE VENDOR IN THE JEMAA EL FNA

▲ DRIED FRUIT STALL

mercilessly, so make sure to ask the price before ordering.

Besides sit-down meals, you'll find exotic snacks on offer too. Over towards the eastern side of the square, a group of stalls offer a food much loved in Morocco — **stewed snails**. The stallholder ladles servings out of a simmering vat, and you eat the snails with a pin or toothpick before slurping back the soup they are stewed in. Just south of the main food stalls are a row of vendors selling **khendenjal**, a hot, spicy infusion based on ginseng and said to be an aphrodisiac. It's usually accompanied by a spicy confection made of flour and ground nuts, and served by the spoonful.

Bars

Grand Hotel Tazi

Corner of Rue Bab Agnaou and Rue el Mouahidine ☎ 044 44 27 87. Daily 9am–midnight. Once, this was the only place in the Medina where you could get a drink, and it's still the cheapest (beers from 20dh). There's nothing fancy about the bar area — squeezed in between the restaurant and the lobby, and frequently spilling over into the latter — but it manages to be neither rough nor pretentious (a rare feat among Marrakesh drinking dens) and women should have no worries about drinking here.

Southern Medina and Agdal gardens

The biggest attractions in the southern half of the Medina are the fabulous ruin of the El Badi Palace and the exquisite Saadian Tombs. Both lie within the Kasbah district, which was originally Marrakesh's walled citadel. To the east of here is the Royal Palace, used by the king when visiting the city (and not open to the public). The area east of this is the Mellah, once Morocco's largest Jewish ghetto; the extensive Agdal gardens lie to the south. Between the Royal Palace and the Jemaa el Fna, the residential Riad Zitoun el Kedim and Riad Zitoun el Jedid quarters are home to two interesting museums and the beautiful Bahia Palace. The southern part of the Medina is less crowded and frenetic than the northern part, broken up by things like the king's palace (which occupies a fair chunk of the area) into more distinct districts such as the Kasbah, the Mellah, and the Berrima and Bab Hmar quarters.

Dar Si Said

Derb Si Said, off Rue Riad Zitoun el Jedid. Daily except Tues 9am–12.15pm & 3–6.15pm. 20dh. A smaller version of the Bahia Palace, Dar Si Said was built in the late nineteenth century for the brother of Bou Ahmed (see p.64) who, like Bou Ahmed himself, became royal chamberlain. It's a pleasing building, with beautiful pooled courtyards, scented with lemons, palms and flowers, and it houses an impressive **Museum of Moroccan Arts**. The museum is particularly strong on eighteenth- and nineteenth-century woodwork, most in cedar. Besides the furniture, there are Berber doors and window frames, all hand-carved in beautifully irregular shapes, and wonderful painted ceilings. There are also (upstairs) a number of traditional wedding **palanquins**, once widely used for carrying the bride, veiled and hidden, to her new home.

Maison Tiskiwin

Derb el Bahia, off Rue Riad Zitoun el Jedid. Daily 9.30am–12.30pm & 3.30–5.30pm. 15dh. The Maison Tiskiwin houses a unique collection of Moroccan and

▼ MAISON TISKIWIN

Saharan artefacts, billed as "a journey from Marrakesh to Timbuktu and back". Furnished from the collection of Dutch anthropologist Bert Flint, the exhibition underlines the longstanding cultural links across the desert, a result of the centuries of **caravan trade** between Morocco and Mali. Each of the rooms features carpets, fabrics, clothes and jewellery from a different region of the Sahara, with explanatory notes in French.

Place des Ferblantiers

This tinsmiths' square, once part of a souk belonging to the Mellah (see p.66), is now dominated by the workshops of **lantern makers**. The area to its north has become quite a pretty little rose garden, while the remainder of the Mellah's souk can be found through a doorway just to the northeast of Place des Ferblantiers.

El Badi Palace

Bab Berrima. Daily 8.30–11.45am & 2.30–5.45pm. 10dh. Sultan Ahmed el Mansour's sixteenth-century El Badi Palace is substantially in ruins, reduced throughout to its red *pisé* walls. However, enough remains to suggest that its name – **"The Incomparable"** – was not entirely immodest.

The original entrance was in the southeast corner, but today you enter from the north, through the **Green Pavilion**, emerging into a vast **central courtyard** over 130m long and nearly as wide. In the northeast corner, you can climb up to get an overview from the ramparts and a closer view of the **storks** nesting atop them.

Within the central courtyard are four sunken gardens, each pair separated by a pool, with

▲ STORK NEST, EL BADI PALACE

smaller pools in the four corners of the courtyard. When filled – as during the June folklore festival (see p.137) – they are an incredibly majestic sight.

You can pay another 10dh to see the original **minbar** (pulpit) from the Koutoubia Mosque (see p.53), housed in a pavilion in the southwest corner of the main courtyard. Once one of the most celebrated works of art in the Muslim world, it was commissioned from the Andalusian capital Cordoba in 1137 and took eight years to complete. The whole structure was covered with the most exquisite inlay work of which, sadly, only patches remain. The minbar was removed from the Koutoubia in 1962 for restoration, and eventually brought here.

South of the courtyard are the ruins of the **palace stables** and, beyond them, leading towards the walls of the present Royal Palace, a series of **dungeons**, used into the last century as a state prison.

The Saadian Tombs

Rue de la Kasbah. Daily 8.30–11.45am & 2.30–5.45pm. 10dh. The tombs of the Saadians – the dynasty

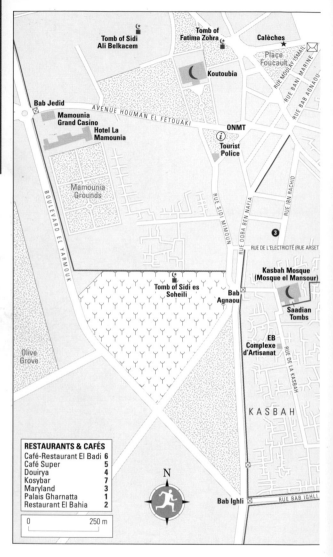

RESTAURANTS & CAFÉS

Café-Restaurant El Badi	6
Café Super	5
Douirya	4
Kosybar	7
Maryland	3
Palais Gharnatta	1
Restaurant El Bahia	2

0   250 m

which ruled Morocco from 1554 to 1669 – escaped plundering by the rapacious Sultan Moulay Ismail, of the subsequent Alaouite dynasty, probably because he feared bad luck if he desecrated them. Instead, he blocked all access bar an obscure entrance from the Kasbah mosque. The tombs lay half-ruined and half-forgotten until they were rediscovered by a French aerial survey in 1917.

The finer of the two **mausoleums** in the enclosure is on the left as you come in

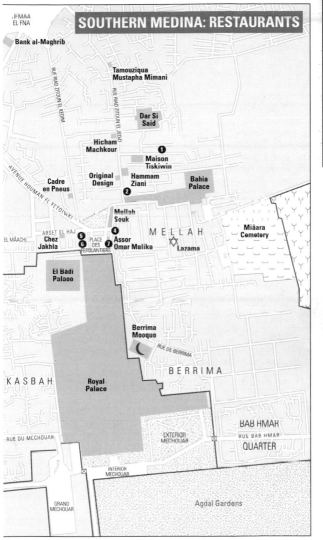

SOUTHERN MEDINA: RESTAURANTS

.IFMAA
EL FNA

Bank al-Maghrib

RUE RIAD ZITOUN EL KEDIM

Tamouziqua
Mustapha Mimani

RUE RIAD ZITOUN EL JEDID

Dar Si
Said

Hicham
Machkour

❶

Maison
Tiskiwin

AVENUE HOUMAN EL FETOUAKI

Cadre
en Pneus

Original
Design

Hammam
Ziani

❷

Bahia
Palace

Mellah
Souk

ARSET EL HAJ

EL MÂACH)

Chez
Jakhla

❺
❻

PLACE
DES
FERBLANTIERS

❹

❼ Assor
Omar Malika

M E L L A H

✡

Lazama

Miâara
Cemetery

El Badi
Palaoo

Berrima
Mooque

RUE DE BERRIMA

B E R R I M A

BAB HMAR

K A S B A H

Royal
Palace

RUE BAB HMAR

QUARTER

RUE DU MECHOUAR

EXTERIOR
MECHOUAR

INTERIOR
MECHOUAR

GRAND
MECHOUAR

Agdal Gardens

– a beautiful group of three rooms. Architecturally, the most important feature here is the **mihrab** (the niche indicating the direction of Mecca), its pointed horseshoe arch supported by an incredibly delicate arrangement of columns. The room itself was originally an oratory, probably not intended for burial use. Opposite the *mihrab*, an elaborate arch leads to the domed central chamber and the tomb of Sultan Ahmed el Mansour, flanked by those of his sons and successors. The room is spectacular, with faint light filtering onto the tombs from an interior lantern placed in a tremendous vaulted roof, and the *zellij* tilework on the walls is full of colour and motion.

It was Ahmed who built the other mausoleum, older and less impressive, above the tombs of his mother and of the Saadian dynasty's founder, Mohammed esh Sheikh. The latter is buried in the inner room – or at least his torso is, since the Turkish mercenaries who murdered him took his head back to Istanbul for public display.

Outside, round the garden and courtyard, are scattered the tombs of over a hundred more Saadian princes and members of the royal household.

Bab Agnaou

This was one of the two original entrances to the Kasbah, but the magnificent blue granite gateway which stands here today was built in 1885. The name

▼ BAB AGNAOU

actually means "black people's gate", a reference to its use by swarthy commoners, while the fair-complexioned aristocracy had their own gateway (now long gone). The entrance is surrounded by concentric arches of decoration and topped with an inscription in decorative script, which reads: "Enter with blessing, serene people."

The Bahia Palace

Rue Riad Zitoun el Jedid. Sat–Thurs 8.45–11.45am & 2.45–5.45pm, Fri 8.45–11.30am & 3–5.45pm. 10dh. The Bahia Palace – its name means "brilliance" – was originally built in 1866–67 for the then grand vizier (akin to a prime minister), **Si Moussa**. In the 1890s it was extended by his son, **Bou Ahmed**, himself a grand vizier and regent to the sultan, who ascended the throne aged 14. There is a certain pathos to the empty, echoing chambers of the palace, and the inevitable passing of Bou Ahmed's influence and glory. When he died, the palace was looted by its staff, and his family driven out to starvation and ruin.

You enter the palace from the west, through an arcaded courtyard. This leads through to a small riad (enclosed garden), part of Bou Ahmed's extension and decorated with beautiful carved stucco and cedarwood surrounds. The adjoining eastern salon leads through to the **great courtyard** of Si Moussa's palace, with a fountain in its centre and vestibules on all sides, each boasting a marvellous painted wooden ceiling.

South of the great courtyard is the large riad, the heart of Si Moussa's palace, fragrant with fruit trees and melodious with birdsong, approaching the very

ideal of beauty in Arabic domestic architecture. The halls to the east and west are decorated with fine *zellij* fireplaces and painted wooden ceilings. From here, you leave the palace via the private apartment built in 1898 for Ahmed's wife, **Lalla Zinab**, where again it's worth looking up to check out the painted ceiling, carved stucco and stained-glass windows.

The Mellah

Set up in 1558, Marrakesh's **Jewish ghetto** was almost a town in itself in the sixteenth century, presided over by rabbis, with its own souks, gardens, fountains and synagogues. Jewish ghettoes in Morocco were called *mellah* (salter), supposedly because residents of the first – in Fes – had the job of salting the decapitated heads of executed criminals for display on the city walls.

The present-day Mellah is almost entirely **Muslim** – most of the Jews left long ago for Casablanca, France or Israel. The quarter is immediately distinct, with taller houses and narrower streets than elsewhere in the Medina. Would-be guides may offer (for a tip, of course) to show you some of the surviving synagogues, notably the **Lazama** (36 Derb R agraga; no sign, just knock on the door; open to the public Sun–Thurs 9am–6pm, Fri 9am–1pm, closed Sat and Jewish hols; there's no charge, but a tip is expected). The synagogue is still in use but the interior is modern and not tremendously interesting. Like

▲ STUCCO AND ZELLIJ TILING AT THE BAHIA PALACE

all the Mellah's synagogues, it forms part of a private house, which you'll notice is decorated with Star-of-David *zellij* tiling.

The **Miâara Jewish cemetery** on the east side of the Mellah (Sun–Thurs 7am–6pm, Fri 7am–3pm, closed Sat and Jewish hols; no charge but tip expected) is reckoned to date from the early seventeenth century. Among the tombs are eleven shrines to Jewish marabouts (*tzadikim*), illustrating an interesting parallel between the Moroccan varieties of Judaism and Islam.

Agdal gardens

Access via the path leading south from the Interior Mechouar; bus #6 from Place Foucault will take you to the path's southern end. Fri & Sun 8am–5pm. Free. These massive gardens, stretching some 3km, and best reached by taxi, are surrounded by walls, with gates (closed) at each of the northern corners, but once out of sight of them, it feels as if you're in the countryside rather than in a city garden. Inside, the orange, fig, lemon, apricot and pomegranate **orchards** are divided into square plots by endless raised walkways and broad avenues of olive trees. The area is watered by an incredible system of wells and **underground channels**, known as *khettera*, that go as far as the base of the Atlas and date, in part, from the very founding of the city.

At the heart of the gardens lies a series of pools, the largest of which is the **Sahraj el Hana** (the Tank of Health – now a green, algae-clogged rectangle of water). Probably dug during Almohad times, the pool is flanked by a ramshackle old **summer pavilion**, where the last few precolonial sultans held picnics and boating parties.

La Mamounia hotel and gardens

Av Bab Jedid. It's worth popping into Marrakesh's top hotel for a pot of tea on the terrace and a look at the opulent interior, with its 1920s Art Deco touches. The terrace overlooks the hotel's **gardens**, which regular visitor Winston Churchill described to his friend Franklin D. Roosevelt – when they were here together in 1943 – as the loveliest spot in the world. Walled off from the outside bustle, yet only a few minutes' walk from the Jemaa el Fna, the gardens were once royal grounds, laid out by the Saadians with a succession of pavilions. Today they're somewhat Europeanized in style but have retained the traditional elements of citrus trees and walkways. Note that visitors are not supposed to enter the hotel wearing shorts or jeans.

Shops

Assor Omar Malika

35 Place des Ferblantiers ☎ 062 60 63 02. Daily 8am–8pm. A big selection of brass and iron lanterns in all shapes and sizes, doubling up as light shades for boring old electric bulbs. The many-pointed star-shaped lanterns with glass panes are a big favourite, as are simple candle-holder lanterns;

▼ LA MAMOUNIA HOTEL

▲ TYRE CRAFTS

there are larger and grander designs too.

Cadre en Pneus

97 Rue Riad Zitoun el Kedim. Sat–Thurs 9am–6.30pm, Fri 9am–1pm. This is one of a group of small shops at this end of the road that recycle disused car tyres. Initially they made hammam supplies such as buckets and flip-flops (try the shops 20m further down towards Place des Ferblantiers for these), but they've since branched out into products such as picture frames and framed mirrors, odd rather than elegant in black rubber, but certainly worth a look. Best buys are the tuffets (stools), which rather resemble giant liquorice allsorts.

Chez Jakhla

29 Arset el Haj. Sat–Thurs 9am–9pm, Fri 9am–noon. The walls and floor here are stacked solid with CDs and cassettes of local and foreign sounds. There's Algerian *raï* and Egyptian pop – the music that dominates Moroccan radio – as well as homegrown *raï* and *chaabi* (folk music), classical Andalusian music deriving originally from Muslim-era Spain, music from Marrakesh's great rival city of Fes and even Moroccan rap.

Entreprise Bouchaib Complexe d'Artisanat

7 Derb Baissi Kasbah, Rue de la Kasbah ☎044 38 18 53, ⓦwww .bouchaib.net. Daily 8.30am–8pm. A massive craftwork department store with a huge range of goods at (supposedly) fixed prices, only slightly higher than what you might pay in the souks. The sales assistants who follow you round are generally quite charming and informative. Carpets are the best buy, at prices ranging from around 2000dh upward (expect to pay 7000dh for a decent-sized one), and with a whole floor devoted to them. There's also a huge selection of jewellery, ceramics, brassware and even furniture.

Hicham Machkour

190 Rue Riad Zitoun el Jedid, ☎065 78 04 94. Daily 9am–7pm. If the leather babouches in the main souk (see p.74) don't wow you, here's a whole different babouche concept in raffia – either alone or in combination with various types of leather, including garishly dyed snakeskin and goatskin. The raffia itself, which is made from straw, is candy-coloured and rather pretty, so these are strictly ladies' babouches, starting at around 60dh for plain raffia and 200dh for raffia-and-skin combinations. You're going to have to haggle.

Original Design

231 Rue Riad Zitoun el Jedid, ☎044 38 22 76, ⓦwww.original-design -mrk.com. Daily 9am–7pm. Modern ceramic designer crockery (their own) in beautiful matching colours is what this shop sells, and at fixed prices. The most

striking pieces are in glowing russet, but there are earth colours and pastels too, as well as a set made in imitation of traditional Berber embroidery. They've also got a few pieces of traditional Fassi pottery (from Fes, that is), more by way of contrast than anything else.

Tamouziqua Mustapha Mimani

84 Kennaria Teoula, off Rue Riad Zitoun el Jedid. Daily 9am–8pm. This small shop specializes in Moroccan musical instruments, most notably drums, which they make themselves in their neighbouring workshop; they also offer lessons in how to play. Additionally they sell the lute-like *ginbris*, which make excellent souvenirs to hang on your wall back home.

Cafés

Café-Restaurant El Badi

Off Place des Ferblantiers by Bab Berrima. Daily 9am–8pm. On a rooftop looking out over Place des Ferblantiers and towards the Mellah, this is one place to get close to the storks nesting on the walls of the El Badi Palace. It serves a limited range of hot and soft drinks, and a modest 80dh set menu of soup, salad and couscous, with a Moroccan sweetmeat for afters.

Café Super

47 Place des Ferblantiers. Daily 7am–9.30pm. The tea and coffee are decent enough, but there's nothing really special about this common-or-garden male-dominated Moroccan café – except that it's a great place to watch televised football with the locals. Any big European matches will certainly be on the

box, as will important Moroccan and African games, attracting avid attention from the clientele. Women, however, may feel conspicuous here, especially inside.

Restaurants

Café Restaurant Maryland

Rue Ibn Rachid. Daily 6am–11pm. Reasonably priced and very tasty Moroccan dishes, including wonderful tajines (the rabbit is especially delicious, with lemon and raisins, but watch out – it may include the head), with tables indoors or out front. Expect to pay around 50–80dh for a three-course meal.

Kosybar

47 Place des Ferblantiers ☎044 38 03 24, ⊛kozibar.tripod.com. Daily noon–3pm & 7pm–1am (salads and drinks served 11am–1am). A stylish restaurant and bar with upstairs terraces overlooking Place des Ferblantiers. They serve sushi, snacks, sandwiches, pasta and salad at lunchtime; for supper you can dine on trendy modern dishes like eggplant strudel with basil, or rabbit profiteroles with honey and marjoram. If you want something less fancy, there's plain old squid ravioli, quail cannelloni, chicken teriyaki or monkfish medallions. Main dishes go for around 150–160dh.

Palais Gharnatta

5–6 Derb el Arsa, off Rue Riad Zitoun el Jedid ☎044 38 96 15, ⊛www .gharnata.com. Daily from 8pm (book before 5pm). Popular with foreign visitors, though unfortunately the food (the 500dh menu features pastilla, couscous, lamb tajine) is merely so-so, and individual diners play second-fiddle to groups. However the decor is splendid, as the building is a magnificently decorated sixteenth-century mansion, with an Italian alabaster fountain at its centre; scenes from *The Return of the Pink Panther* were shot here. Past patrons have included Jacqueline Kennedy and the Aga Khan.

Restaurant Douirya

14 Derb Jedid, near Place des Ferblantiers ☎ 044 38 38 36, ⓦ www.restaurantdouirya.com. Daily noon–3pm & 8pm–midnight. *Douirya* means "small house", but this is in fact a palatial establishment with a remarkable painted wooden ceiling. Open for lunch (à la carte or 300dh menu) and dinner (menus at 300dh or 420dh), when there's also music and belly dancing. Specialities include *mechoui* (roast lamb), and pigeon stuffed with honey and almonds. Easy to find, in the southeast corner of a square by the Place des Ferblantiers.

Restaurant El Bahia

1 Rue Riad Zitoun el Jedid, by the Bahia Palace ☎ 044 37 86 79. Daily 8–10pm. A beautifully restored palatial mansion usually offering set menus based on Marrakesh specialties (beef and prune tajine, *couscous aux sept legumes* or *chakchouka*; 350dh) or Fes ones (pastilla of course, or chicken tajine with olive and preserved lemon; 380dh). There's music and dancing to keep you entertained while you eat. Out of season (in Feb and Nov), there's a more modest 200dh menu and no entertainment.

Casino

Grand Casino

Hotel La Mamounia, Av Houman el Fetouaki. Daily 3pm–4am (gaming tables from 9pm). Walking in from the Medina, you'll find this grand, high class casino pretty surreal. Under huge chandeliers and Art Deco glass panels, you can gamble your life savings on roulette, craps or blackjack, or feed your change to the slot machines. Entrance is free, but scruffy clothes, jeans and trainers aren't permitted; men need a jacket and tie to enter the main part of the casino.

▼ MUSICAL INSTRUMENTS

The Northern Medina

The northern part of the Medina starts with the bustling main souk area, beyond which stretches a vast residential area with more workaday shops (grocery stores, everyday clothes shops, hardware merchants and the like) and few tourists. The main area of souks, or markets, which is great for souvenir shopping, is centred on a main thoroughfare, Souk Smarine. Originally, each souk was clearly defined, with one street selling this and another selling that, though these distinctions have now blurred somewhat. Among the most interesting souks are the Rahba Kedima, with its apothecary stalls, and the dyers' souk, hung with brightly coloured hanks of freshly dyed wool. North of the souks are the small but architecturally important Almoravid Koubba, the Marrakesh Museum and the beautifully decorated Ben Youssef Medersa. Beyond, in all directions, are the ordinary residential quarters of the Medina.

Souk Smarine

Busy and crowded, Souk Smarine is an important thoroughfare, covered along its whole course by an **iron trellis** that restricts the sun to shafts of light dappling everything beneath, especially in the early afternoon. Historically the street was dominated by the sale of textiles and clothing. Today, classier tourist "bazaars" are moving in, with American Express signs in the windows, but there are still dozens of

▼ SCARVES IN THE SOUK SMARINE

▲ RAHBA KEDIMA

shops in the arcades selling and tailoring traditional shirts and kaftans. Other shops specialize in multicoloured cotton skullcaps and in **fezzes** (*tarbouche fassi* in Arabic), whose name derives from the city of Fes in northern Morocco, where they originate. The feeling of being in a labyrinth of hidden treasures is heightened by the passages among the shops, leading through to small covered markets. The occasional stucco-covered doorways between shops are entrances to mosques, havens of spiritual refreshment amid the bustle.

Rahba Kedima

Souk Smarine narrows just before the fork at its northern end. The passageways to the right (east) here give a glimpse of the Rahba Kedima, an open marketplace with stalls in the middle and around the outside.

Immediately to the right as you go in is **Souk Btana**, where whole sheepskin pelts are displayed and laid out to dry on the roof. Most interesting, however, are the **apothecary stalls** in the southwest corner of the square, selling **traditional cosmetics** – earthenware saucers of cochineal (*kashiniah*) for lip-rouge, powdered *kohl* eyeliner (traditionally antimony trisulphide, but nowadays more commonly lead sulphide – both are toxic), henna (the only cosmetic unmarried Moroccan women are supposed to use)

Haggling

When buying crafts in the souk, you're expected to haggle. This is as much a way of passing the time of day as a form of hard bargaining, and should be good-natured, not acrimonious. Haggling is a bit like an auction in that you should never start bidding for something if you are not really interested in it, and having offered a price, you are obliged to pay it if the seller agrees. Always have in mind a price you would like to pay and an absolute maximum before you start to haggle. It's also good to note that the shopkeeper's opening price is not necessarily a guide to how low he will drop – each shop is different; while one may go as low as ten percent of the original quote, others may not budge much at all. Ultimately, the question is, how much are you willing to pay? To get an idea of the going rates, you may wish to check fixed-price establishments such as the Ensemble Artisanal (p.81) or Entreprise Bouchaib (p.67).

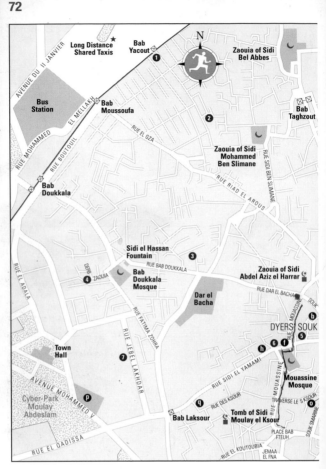

and sticks of *suek* (walnut root or bark) for cleaning teeth. The stalls also sell herbal and animal ingredients still in widespread use for protection against – or the making of – magic spells, roots and tablets for aphrodisiacs, dried pieces of lizard and stork, fragments of beaks and talons and even gazelle horns.

La Criée Berbère

Until the French occupied the city in 1912, La Criée Berbère (the Berber auction) was the site of **slave auctions**, held just before sunset every Wednesday, Thursday and Friday. Most of the slaves had been kidnapped and marched here with the camel caravans from Guinea and Sudan – those too weak to make it were left to die en route. You'll be pleased to know that only rugs and carpets are sold here nowadays.

Kissaria

A covered market at the heart of the souk area, the Kissaria was

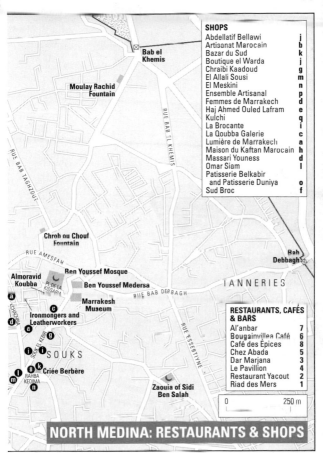

SHOPS

Abdellatif Bellawi	j
Artisanat Marocain	b
Bazar du Sud	k
Boutique el Warda	j
Chraibi Kaadoud	g
El Allali Sousi	m
El Meskini	n
Ensemble Artisanal	p
Femmes de Marrakech	d
Haj Ahmed Ouled Lafram	e
Kulchi	q
La Brocante	c
La Qoubba Galerie	a
Lumière de Marrakech	h
Maison du Kaftan Marocain	d
Massari Youness	l
Omar Siam	
Patisserie Belkabir and Patisserie Duniya	o
Sud Broc	f

RESTAURANTS, CAFÉS & BARS

Al'anbar	7
Bougainvillea Café	6
Café des Épices	8
Chez Abada	5
Dar Marjana	3
Le Pavillion	4
Restaurant Yacout	2
Riad des Mers	1

NORTH MEDINA: RESTAURANTS & SHOPS

originally set up as the market for rich imported **fabrics**. It remains the centre for cloth and clothing, offering an array of beautiful dresses, flowing headscarves and roll upon roll of fine material.

Souk Sabbaghine

The Souk Sabbaghine (or Souk des Teinturiers, the **dyers' souk**), is west of the Kissaria and very near the sixteenth-century Mouassine Mosque and fountain. On a good day, it has a splendid array of freshly dyed sheaves of wool in a multitude of colours hung out to dry. At other times you'll barely see any at all, though you can still take a look as the dyers boil up their tints and prepare the wool for treatment.

Souk Haddadine and Souk Cherratine

It's easy to locate Souk Haddadine, the **ironmongers' souk**, by ear – just head towards the source of the bangings

▲ MARRAKESH SOUK

dynasty, whose style lies at the root of all Moroccan architecture. The windows on each side exhibit the classic shapes of Moroccan design – as do the merlons (the Christmas-tree-like battlements), the complex ribs on the outside of the dome, and the dome's interior support, a sophisticated device of a square and star-shaped octagon, which is itself repeated at each of its corners. Among the remains of the attendant facilities are a large water cistern and latrines and fountains for washing before prayer, much like those adjoining many Moroccan mosques today. Indeed the Almoravid Koubba was probably an ablutions repetition annexe to the **Ben Youssef Mosque** opposite, which, like almost all the Almoravids' buildings, was demolished and rebuilt by the succeeding Almohad dynasty.

and clangings as the artisans shape raw metal into decorative window grilles, lampstands and furniture. Close at hand you'll find Souk Cherratine, the **leatherworkers' souk**, full of workshops where hats, slippers and other goods are cut and stitched by hand, plus specialist shops whose sole occupation is to grind and sharpen tools.

The Almoravid Koubba

On the south side of Place de la Kissaria. Daily: April–Sept 9am–7pm; Oct–March 9am–6pm. 10dh; combined ticket with the Marrakesh Museum 40dh; combined ticket with the Marrakesh Museum and Ben Youssef Medersa 60dh. Situated well below today's ground level, the Almoravid Koubba (correctly called the Koubba Ba'adyin) doesn't look like much, but this small, two-storey structure is the only building in Morocco to survive intact from the eleventh-century Almoravid

The Marrakesh Museum

Place de la Kissaria. Daily: April–Sept 9am–7pm; Oct–March 9am–6pm. 40dh (includes entry to Almoravid Koubba); combined ticket with Ben Youssef Medersa 60dh. This building was once a magnificent late-nineteenth-century palace built for defence minister Mehdi Mnebb, later Morocco's ambassador in London. Neglected for many years, it was restored and opened in 1997 as a museum to house exhibitions of Moroccan **art and sculpture**, both traditional (in the main hall and surrounding rooms), and contemporary (in what were the palace kitchens). It is the building itself, however, that is most memorable, especially the warren of rooms that was once the **hammam**, and the now-covered **inner courtyard** with its huge brass lamp hung above a central fountain. There's also a small café and bookshop in the entrance courtyard.

The Ben Youssef Medersa

Off Place de la Kissaria. Daily. April–Sept 9am–7pm; Oct–March 9am–6pm. 30dh; combined ticket with Marrakesh Museum and Almoravid Koubba 60dh.

Just north of the Marrakesh Museum is the Ben Youssef Medersa, a **religious school** where students learned the Koran by rote. Attached to the neighbouring Ben Youssef Mosque, the medersa was founded under one of Morocco's most illustrious rulers, the "Black Sultan" Abou el Hassan (ruled 1331–49) of the Merenid dynasty. In the 1560s it was almost completely rebuilt under their successors the Saadians, whose intricate, Andalusian-influenced art dominates it. The central courtyard, its carved **cedar lintels** weathered almost flat on the most exposed side, is unusually large. Along two sides run wide, sturdy, columned

arcades, and above them are some of the windows of the dormitory quarters, which are reached by stairs from the entry vestibule. In the **prayer hall**, at the far end of the main court, the decoration is at its best preserved and most elaborate. Notable here, as in the courtyard's cedar carving, is a predominance of pinecone and palm motifs, especially around the *mihrab* (the horseshoe-arched niche indicating the direction of prayer), where their clear protrusion from the rest of the frieze is a rarity in Moroccan stuccowork. The inscriptions are quotations from the Koran, the most common being its opening invocation: "In the name of God, the Compassionate, the Merciful".

▼ THE MARRAKESH MUSEUM

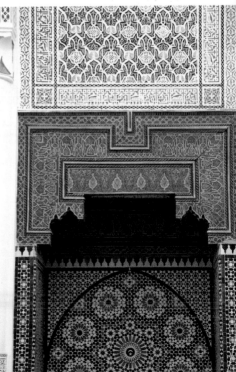

MEDERSA BEN YOUSSEF

▲ MAN OUTSIDE THE BEN YOUSSEF MEDERSA

Almost opposite the entrance to the Ben Youssef Medersa is the **Dar Bellarj**, a house built in the 1930s on the site of a *fondouk*. Now a cultural centre, with a small exhibition on irrigation, it's of no special interest, but charges passing tourists for entry as if it were.

Zaouia of Sidi Abdel Aziz el Harrar

Rue Mouassine. Sidi Abdel Aziz el Harrar (d.1508) was an Islamic scholar who – unusually among Marrakesh's Seven Saints (see box, p.77) – was actually born in Marrakesh, though he made his name in Fes. Among the Seven Saints' shrines, his *zaouia* is one of the smallest, but like the others it has a distinctive red and yellow pattern around the top, just below the roof, indicating that it is part of the pilgrimage circuit established here in the seventeenth century.

Dar el Bacha

Rue Dar el Bacha. Mon–Fri 9am–2pm. 10dh. Also called Dar el Glaoui, this was the palace of **T'hami el Glaoui**, the despotic tribal leader – loved and feted by Europeans, feared and hated by Marrakshis – who ruled Marrakesh on behalf of the French during the colonial period; his extravagances were as legendary as his cruelty. When he died in 1956, a mob ransacked the palace. Nowadays the building is used by the Ministry of Culture, but it was being renovated at last check,

Fondouks

One of the most characteristic types of building in the Medina is the **fondouk** or caravanserai. Originally, *fondouks* were inns used by visiting merchants for storage and lodging when they were in Marrakesh to trade in its souks. All the *fondouks* have a courtyard in the middle surrounded by what were originally stables, while the upper level contains rooms which would have accommodated the merchants. They can be recognized by the upper gallery of rooms around the central courtyard.

Today the *fondouks* are in varying states of repair; some have become private residences, others commercial premises. The doors to the courtyards are usually left open, and no one seems to mind if you wander in to have a look. Some *fondouks* date back to Saadian times (1520–1669), and boast fine woodcarving or stuccowork. There's a row of interesting *fondouks* on the south side of Rue Bab Debbagh, behind the Ben Youssef Medersa, and a whole series along Rue Amesfah, north of the Ben Youssef Mosque, as well as one directly opposite the Chrob ou Chouf fountain.

The Seven Saints of Marrakesh

Some two hundred holy men and women, known as **marabouts**, are buried in Marrakesh. Although the idea is considered slightly dubious in orthodox Islam, it's widely believed that praying to God at the tomb of a marabout attracts a special *beraka* (blessing). A marabout's tomb may thus become the centrepiece of a mosque-mausoleum called a **zaouia**, often the focus for a brotherhood of the marabout's followers, who usually belong to the mystic branch of Islam known as **Sufism**.

Marrakesh's seven most prominent marabouts, usually referred to in English as the "Seven Saints" of the city, have little in common aside from being buried here. One of them, Sidi Mohammed Ben Slimane, never even lived in Marrakesh – his body was brought here after his death. The most prominent, Sidi Bel Abbes, has become pretty much the city's patron saint.

You'd have to be pretty dedicated, and a Muslim, to do the tour of the seven saints' mausoleums (non-Muslims are not allowed to enter), but you can certainly see all the tombs from the outside, and a couple – Sidi Bel Abbes (p.79) and Sidi Abdel Aziz el Harrar (see p.76) – are definitely worth a second look.

and will open to the public when work is completed (supposedly in the next year or so).

Bab Doukkala Mosque

Rue Bab Doukkala. Serving the lively Bab Doukkala quarter, this *pisé* mosque with its elegant brick minaret was constructed in 1557–58 on the orders of Lalla Messaouda, mother of the Ahmed el Mansour, the most illustrious sultan of the Saadian dynasty. It is said that she originally intended to have it built in a different quarter, but residents managed to divert the builders and their materials to this site instead. On the main street in front of the mosque is the impressive three-bayed **Sidi el Hassan fountain**, now converted into a small art gallery.

Chrob ou Chouf Fountain

Rue Assouel, a little way north of Place de la Kissaria. This small sixteenth-century recessed fountain (its name means "drink and admire") is mainly notable for its carved cedar lintel,

incorporating calligraphy and stalactite-like projections. Back in the days before people had running water at home, paying to put up a fountain was a pious act of charity, sanctioned by the Koran. Religious institutions and wealthy philanthropists had them installed to provide not only drinking water, but also a place to wash – most notably to perform the ritual ablutions demanded by the Koran before

▼ CHROB OU CHOUF FOUNTAIN

prayer, which is why so many of the surviving fountains are attached to mosques.

Zaouia of Sidi Ben Salah

Place Ben Salah. This fourteenth-century holy man's tomb is one of the few important buildings in the Medina to have been put up under the Merenid dynasty, who had moved the Moroccan capital from Marrakesh to its rival city of Fes. The most prominent feature is the handsome **minaret**, covered with brilliant green tiles in a *darj w ktarf* pattern (see p.53). The square in front of the *zaouia* is usually pretty lively with fruit and vegetable sellers and other traders, and gives a flavour of Medina life without tourism.

The tanneries

Along and off Rue Bab Debbagh. Head east along Rue Bab Debbagh and you'll notice a rather unpleasant whiff in the air as you near the city gate, indicating the proximity of the tanneries. One tannery that's easy to find is on the north side of the street about 200m before Bab Debbagh, opposite

the blue-tiled stand-up fountain, with another one about 200m further west.

The tanneries were sited at the edge of the city not only because of the smell, but also for access to water: a stream, the Oued Issil, runs just outside the walls. If you want to take a closer look at the **tanning process**, come in the morning, when the cooperatives are at work. The smell comes largely from the first stage, where the hides are soaked in a vat of pigeon droppings. The natural dyes traditionally used to colour the leather have largely been replaced by chemicals, many of them carcinogenic – a fact to remember when you see people standing waist-deep in them.

Bab Debbagh

Among the more interesting of Marrakesh's city gates, Bab Debbagh is supposedly Almoravid in design, though over the years it must have been almost totally rebuilt. Passing through the gate, you become aware of its very real defensive purpose: three internal **chicanes** are placed in such

▼ THE TANNERIES

a manner as to force anyone attempting to storm it to make several turns. Just before the gate, several shops on the left give good **views** over the tanneries from their roofs. Shopkeepers may invite you up, but agree the price first or you'll be mercilessly overcharged. Bus #5 outside the gate runs to and from the Koutoubia.

Bab el Khemis

This beautiful gate, originally Almoravid though rebuilt under the Almohads, is surrounded by concentric rings of decoration and topped with Christmas-tree-like castellations. Its name, meaning "Thursday Gate", is a reference to the market held outside, 300m to the north, past a marabout's tomb and a former cemetery, now landscaped as a little park. You'll find stalls out most days, but the main market is held on Thursday (in the morning). It's mainly a local produce market, though the odd handicraft item does occasionally surface. Bus #5 connects Bab el Khemis with the Koutoubia.

Zaouia of Sidi Bel Abbes

Rue Bab Taghzout. The most important of Marrakesh's seven saints, **Sidi Bel Abbes** (b.1130) was a prolific performer of miracles, particularly famed for giving sight to the blind. The huge mosque that now houses his tomb, with a green-tiled roof and surrounding outbuildings, dates largely from an early eighteenth century reconstruction. It lies just north of **Bab Taghzout**, which was one of the gates of the Medina

▲ BAB DEBBAGH

until the eighteenth century, when Sultan Mohammed Abdallah extended the walls north to include the Sidi Bel Abbes quarter. As with all *zaouias*, non-Muslims are not allowed to enter the complex but may take a look in from the outside. The foundation which runs the *zaouia* also owns much of the surrounding quarter and is engaged in charitable work, distributing food each evening to the blind.

Shops

Abdellatif Bellawi

56 & 103 Kissariat Lossta, between Souk el Kebir and Souk Attarine. Sat–Thurs 9am–6.30pm, Fri 9am–1pm. Beads and bangles, yes, but a great selection and some lovely stuff. The bangles – mostly Berber from the Atlas – are chunky solid silver, while the beads range from traditional Berber necklaces, originating in the Atlas and the Sahara, to West African money beads, beads made of pebbles and

shells and necklaces from as far away as Yemen. There are more frivolous items too, like the cowrie-encrusted Gnaoua caps hanging up outside the door, plus rings, earrings and woollen Berber belts.

Artisanat Marocain

16–18 Souk Brâadia. Daily 10am–6pm. The thuya (also spelt *thuja*) tree, which grows across the south of Morocco, is much prized: not only the wood but also the rootstock is hand-carved into beautiful sculptures, boxes and furniture, all sold here. Among the more popular items are chess and backgammon boards (inlaid with the yellow wood of citrus trees, and the same dyed black), solitaire sets and wooden jewel boxes. There are also some very elegant CD racks, and some great – in quality and scale – tables and chests. The boxes, incidentally, smell as good as they look – open one up and have a sniff.

Bazar du Sud

14 & 117 Souk des Tapis ☎044 44 30 04. Daily 8.30am–6.30pm.

Carpets, carpets and more carpets from all over the south of Morocco. Most are claimed to be old (if you prefer them spanking new, pop next door to Bazar Jouti at nos. 16 & 119), and most are coloured with wonderful natural dyes such as saffron (yellow), cochineal (red) and indigo (blue). A large carpet could cost 2000dh, but you might be able to find a small rug for around 500dh.

Boutique el Warda

44 Kissariat Lossta, between Souk el Kebir and Souk Attarine. Daily 9am–9pm. Up Souk el Kebir (on the corner of the third alley on the left if you're heading north from the fork with Souk Attarine) is this little shop selling scarves of cotton or silk – white and frilly, tie-dyed or plain. There's no sign, but it's the first shop in the Kissaria as you turn in from Souk el Kebir – look for the scarves and you'll see it soon enough (though the next shop along and the one opposite both sell scarves too). Prices start at 10dh.

▼ SPICE SHOP

Chraïbi Kaadoud

2 Souk Serrajine, off Souk el Kebir ☎044 44 37 62. Daily except Fri 8am–8pm. In theory this is a shop that sells saddles for horses, but part of the traditional saddle is a layer of woollen felt, and as a sideline, they've started producing felt bags, hats, rugs, even beads, each item made in a single piece with a big splash of colour. Not your average Medina craft and well worth a look. Bags go for 220dh, rugs for 400dh.

El Aliali Sousi

125 Souk Smarine, opposite the alley to Rahba Kedima. Daily 8.30am–8.30pm. This little place sells silver – old and new – whether in the form of jewellery, old coins, spoons and ladles, or just odd little curiosities (some in other metals, such as brass). Pricey, but it's worth popping in for a browse.

El Meskini

152 Rahba Kedima, on the south side of the square. Daily 7am–10pm. Among the assorted apothecary shops on the south and west side of the Rahba Kedima, this one stands out for two reasons: firstly, it doesn't sell dubious animal products. The second reason is that the genial owner will patiently explain the wondrous properties of all the herbs, spices and scents he sells.

Ensemble Artisanal

Av Mohammed V, midway between the Koutoubia and Bab Nkob ☎044 38 66 74. Mon–Sat 8.30am–7pm, Sun 8.30am–1pm. This government-run complex of small arts and crafts shops holds a reasonable range of goods, notably leather, textiles and carpets. Shopping here is hassle-free, and the prices, which are more or less fixed, are a good gauge of the going rate if you intend to bargain elsewhere. At the back are a dozen or so workshops where you can watch young people learning a range of crafts including carpet-weaving.

Femmes de Marrakech

67 Souk el Kchachbia, west of the Almoravid Koubba. Daily 9am–1pm & 3–7.30pm. A cooperative of nine women run this little dress shop, creating their own garments, and also selling – on a fair-trade basis – clothes made at home by other women. The dresses are handmade from pure cotton and linen fabrics in a mix of Moroccan and Western styles. Colours range from sober pinks and greys to bright orange tie-dye, and there are some great *gandoras* (sleeveless kaftans) with hand-sewn multicoloured tassles.

Haj Ahmed Ouled Lafram

49–51 Souk Smata (Souk Principal des Babouches). Daily except Fri 9am–6pm. There are any number of shops in this souk selling traditional Moroccan slippers – worn with the back pushed down – but while neighbouring emporiums specialize in newfangled designs, Haj Ahmed sticks mainly to the classic leather slipper, though with some tasteful variations – a pleasantly subdued grey for example, among other assorted colours – and some less tasteful ones, including a truly horrible snakeskin version. Prices start at around 100dh.

Kulchi

1 Rue des Ksour ☎062 64 97 83. Daily 9.30am–1pm & 3–7pm. Moroccan clothes for Western women is what this rather chic little boutique sells. The range isn't huge, but there are slinky

kaftans, T-shirts with Moroccan-inspired designs, and diaphanous housecoats. Accessories include handbags made from flour sacks and other recycled materials.

La Brocante

16 Souk Souaffine, off Souk el Kebir. Daily 10am–1pm & 3–6.30pm. A little shop with all sorts of antique curiosities: toys, watches, medals, enamelled metal signs and what would be just bric-a-brac, but for the fact that it's clearly been chosen with a tasteful eye.

La Qoubba Galerie

91 Souk Châaria ☎044 38 05 18, ⓦwww.art-gallery-marrakech.com. Daily 9am–6pm. Paintings and sculptures by contemporary Marrakshi artists are displayed in an attractive little two-room gallery off Place de la Kissaria, with a second branch at 115 Souk el Hanna. The *qoubba* (dome) after which it's named surmounts the building behind.

Lumière de Marrakech

14 Souk des Feroniers ☎067 23 86 02. Daily 9am–6pm. Lampholders, lampshades and screens in wrought iron, which the ironmongers will make to order right there in front of you. They're a little bit heavy to cart home, but they do have a certain clunky elegance. The neighbouring shops offer alternative designs.

Maison du Kaftan Marocain

65 Rue Sidi el Yumani ☎044 44 10 51. Daily 9am–8pm. All sorts of robes, tunics and kaftans in this wonderful shop, from see-through glittery gowns and sequinned velvet tunics to lush embroidered silk kaftans that make sumptuous housecoats (except that they go for prices in excess of 2000dh). Most are for women, but there are also a few men's garments. Past customers include Jean-Paul Gautier and Samuel L. Jackson, as photos on the wall testify.

Massari Youness

53 & 63 Souk el Kchachbia, west of the Almoravid Koubba ☎044 44 15 97. Daily 10am–7.30pm. The speciality at no. 63 is mirrors, framed

▼ MAISON DU KAFTAN MAROCAIN

▲ MOROCCAN PASTRIES

with mosaics of coloured glass. Costing 100dh and up, they're a little kitsch, to be sure, but sweetly so. Across the street at no. 53, the same people run a shop selling candles, and also wax candle boxes (you put a candle inside and the box glows, remaining solid because it's made of wax with a higher melting point than the candle).

Omar Siam
39 Souk Nejjarine, part of Souk el Kebir. Daily 8am–7pm. It's not much more than a hole in the wall, but stop for a peek at Omar Siam's range of wooden spoons, handmade in all sizes, and really quite charming in their own small way. There are ladles for eating *harira*, smaller ones for measuring spices, spoons that you could stir your tea with, spoons with holes for fishing olives out of brine, and non-spoon items too: pastry moulds for making Moroccan sweets, and even pairs of wooden scissors (for cutting fresh pasta, in case you wondered). The smallest things are just 5dh.

Patisserie Belkabir and Patisserie Duniya
63–65 Souk Smarine, by the corner of Traverse el Ksour. Daily 8am–8pm. Side by side, these shops specialize in traditional Moroccan sweetmeats, stuffed with nuts and drenched in syrup, and particularly popular during the holy month of Ramadan, when of course they are eaten by night. A kilo of assorted sticky delights will set you back 100dh.

Sud Broc
65 Rue Mouassine. Daily 9am–7.30pm. A bric-a-brac shop, not as good as *La Brocante* (see p.82), and with quite high prices (bargain hard), but it does have an interesting selection, including old cameras, watches, lighters – Zippos and imitation Zippos, old and new – and other relics of the good old days.

Cafés

Bougainvillea Café
33 Rue Mouassine ☎ 044 44 11 11, ⊛ www.bougainvilleacafe.com. Daily 10am–10.30pm. An upmarket café and quiet retreat in the middle of the Medina; handy for a break after a hard morning's shopping in the souks. Set in a secluded patio, it tries hard to be

stylish, and generally succeeds, the lack of actual bougainvillea flowers being made up for by bougainvillea-coloured paintwork and chairs. There are salads, sandwiches, cakes, juices, coffee and tea – including tea flavoured with mountain herbs from the Atlas – but most of all it's a pleasant space to relax in, doubling as an art gallery, with exhibits by a different local painter each month.

Café des Épices

Place Rahba Kedima (north side). Daily: winter 9am–6pm; summer 9am–8pm. A small café offering refuge from the hubbub, with orange juice, mint tea, coffee in various permutations, including spiced with cinnamon, and views over the Rahba Kedima from the upper floor and the roof terrace.

▼ CAFÉ DES ÉPICES

Chez Abada

12 Souk des Teinturiers. Daily 8am–5.30pm. The only thing that makes this otherwise bog-standard little café worth a stop is its covered roof terrace. This gives a view over the rooftops above the dyers' souk, where freshly dyed wool and cloth is hung out to dry, resplendent in its many colours. You'll be charged double the usual price for a coffee if you take it on the roof terrace, but as the usual price is only 5dh, it doesn't really matter very much.

Restaurants

Dar Marjana

15 Derb Sidi Ali Tair, off Rue Bab Doukkala ☎ 044 38 51 10. Daily except Tues from 8pm. Advance booking only. This restaurant is housed in an early nineteenth-century palace, said by some to be the most beautiful in the Medina. Look for the sign above the entrance to a passageway diagonally across the street from the corner of the Dar el Glaoui; take the passage and look for the green door facing you before a right turn. Among the tasty dishes they serve, two classics stand out: pastilla, a poultry (traditionally pigeon) pie spiced with cinnamon, originating from Fes in northern Morocco, and *couscous aux sept legumes*. The set menu costs 660dh.

Le Pavillion

47 Derb Zaouia ☎ 044 38 70 40. Daily except Tues from 7.30pm, in summer also noon–2.30pm. Best approached from Rue Bab Doukkala, round the back of the Bab Doukkala Mosque – look for the sign over the first archway on the right, head down the passage and it's the last door on the right. The

restaurant is in a beautifully restored middle-class residence, with a tree-shaded patio and Berber wall hangings. Among the specialities whipped up by Michelin-starred French chef Laurent Tarridec are lobster ravioli and a Grand Marnier soufflé. At around 300–400dh à la carte, it's more than worth the price.

Restaurant Yacout

79 Sidi Ahmed Soussi ☎044 38 29 00 or 29. Daily except Mon 8pm–midnight. In a gorgeous old palace, the *Yacout* opened as a restaurant in 1987 with columns and fireplaces in super-smooth orange- and blue-striped *tadelakt* plaster, courtesy of American interior designer and Marrakesh resident Bill Willis. The owner, Mohammad Zkhiri, is also Marrakesh's British consul. The easiest way to get there is by *petit taxi* – the driver will usually walk you to the door. After a drink on the roof terrace, you move down into one of the intimate salons surrounding the courtyard for a selection of salads, followed by a tajine, then lamb couscous and (if you have room) dessert. The classic Moroccan tajine of chicken with preserved lemon and olive is a favourite here, but the fish tajine is also rated very highly. The cuisine has in the past received Michelin plaudits, though standards are beginning to slip as the tour groups move in. Booking ahead is advised.

The menu costs 700dh per person.

Riad des Mers

411 Derb Sidi Messaoud ☎044 37 53 04. Daily except Mon noon–2pm & 8pm–midnight. They bring their own supplies in from the coast for this French fish and seafood restaurant in a patio garden (covered in winter), run by the proprietors of the neighbouring *Riad Sindibad* (see p.123). You can start with oysters or razor shells, continue with sea bass, king prawns or monkfish *brochettes*, and finish with chocolate pudding (admittedly not very French, nor very fishy, but very tasty nonetheless). A starter, main course and dessert will cost you 120dh at lunchtime, 245dh in the evening.

Bars

Al'anbar

47 Rue Jebel Lakhdar. Daily 8pm–3am. Expensive imported liquors line the wall behind the bar here, which consists of a huge balcony overlooking the dining area, as a theatre's upper circle might overlook the stalls. It's best to turn up late in the evening when the place is packed out and the dining area becomes a dancefloor, though earlier on, the floor is used for the dinner entertainment spectacle – a belly dancer with light show, which you might enjoy.

The Ville Nouvelle and Palmery

The downtown area of the Ville Nouvelle is Guéliz, whose main thoroughfare, Avenue Mohammed V, runs all the way down to the Koutoubia. It's in Guéliz that you'll find the the more upmarket shops and most of Marrakesh's nightlife. South of Guéliz, the Hivernage district was built as a garden suburb; it's where most of the city's newer tourist hotels are located. Though the Ville Nouvelle is hardly chock-a-block with attractions, it does have one must-see: the Majorelle Garden, east of Guéliz and just northwest of the Medina. West of Hivernage, the Menara gardens are less compelling, but they host an evening spectacle featuring fireworks and dancers. Otherwise, you can get a peaceful respite from the full-on activity of Marrakesh's streets by heading to the palmery, or oasis, just outside the city.

Majorelle Garden (Jardin Bou Saf)

Off Av Yacoub el Mansour. Daily 8am–6pm. 30dh; no dogs or unaccompanied children allowed.

▼ THE MAJORELLE GARDEN

The Majorelle Garden is a meticulously planned twelve-acre botanical garden, created in the 1920s and 1930s by French painter **Jacques Majorelle** (1886–1962), and now owned by fashion designer **Yves Saint Laurent**. The feeling of tranquillity here is enhanced by verdant groves of bamboo, dwarf palm and agave, the cactus garden and the various lily-covered pools. The pavilion is painted in a striking cobalt blue – the colour of French workmen's overalls, so Majorelle claimed – though it seems to have improved in the Moroccan light.

In Majorelle's former studio, the **Museum of Islamic Arts** (15dh) exhibits Saint Laurent's fine personal collection of North African carpets, pottery, furniture and doors, and has one room devoted to Majorelle's engravings and paintings.

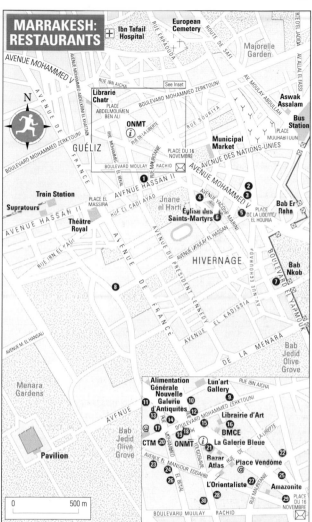

RESTAURANTS, CAFÉS, BARS & CLUBS

Menara gardens

Av de la Menara. Daily 8am–6pm.
Free. A popular picnic spot for
Marrakshi families, the Menara
gardens couldn't be simpler to
find: just follow the road from
Bab Jedid, the gateway by the
Hotel La Mamounia. Like the
Agdal gardens (see p.65), the
Menara was restored and its
pavilions rebuilt in the mid-
nineteenth century, though
unlike the Agdal it is more
olive grove than orchard. (If
you want to get the feel of a
true olive plantation, go to the
nearby **Bab Jedid olive grove**,
which makes a worthwhile stop
on your way to or from the
Menara.)

At night, except in January
and February, the pool becomes
the scene for a **Marvels and
Reflections** show (Mon–Sat
10pm, daily in April, May and
August; 250dh or 400dh),
featuring fireworks, dancers
and acrobats. The ticket office
(daily 9am–8pm) is at the
park entrance; for further
information, call ☎044 43 95
80. Should you want to get
up on a camel for a little spin,
there's usually someone by the
park entrance offering rides.

Avenue Mohammed V

Named after the king who
presided over Morocco's
independence from France,
Avenue Mohammed V is
Marrakesh's main artery. It's
on and around this boulevard
that you'll find the city's main
concentration of upmarket
shops, restaurants and smart
pavement cafés, and its junctions
form the Ville Nouvelle's main
centres of activity: **Place de
la Liberté**, with its modern
fountain; **Place 16 Novembre**,
by the main post office; and
**Place Abdelmoumen Ben
Ali**, epicentre of Marrakesh's
modern shopping zone. Looking
back along Avenue Mohammed
V from Guéliz to the Medina,
on a clear day at least, you
should see the Koutoubia rising
in the distance, with the Atlas
mountains behind.

Théâtre Royal

40 Av de la France ☎044 43 15 16.
Daily 8.30am–7pm. Free. With its
Classical portico and dome,
designed by Morocco's leading
architect, **Charles Boccara**,
this is the most impressive piece
of new architecture in the Ville
Nouvelle. As well as a theatre, it
has a hall exhibiting paintings
and sculpture by local artists.

Église des Saints-Martyrs

Rue de l'Imam Ali ☎044 43 05 85.
No fixed hours. Free. Marrakesh's
Catholic church, built in 1930,
could easily be a
little church in rural
France, but for its
distinctly Marrakshi
red-ochre hue. The
church is dedicated
to six Franciscan
friars who insisted
on preaching
Christianity on the
city's streets in the
year 1220. When
the sultan ordered
them to either

▼ MARVELS AND REFLECTIONS SHOW, MENARA GARDENS

▲ THÉÂTRE ROYAL

desist or leave, they refused, and were promptly beheaded, to be canonized by the Church in 1481.

The European cemetery

Rue Erraouda Daily: Oct–March 8am–6pm; April–Sept 7am–7pm Free. Opened in 1925, this is a peaceful plot with lots of wild flowers, and some quite Poe-esque French family mausoleums. The first thing you'll notice on entry is the large white obelisk dedicated to the soldiers who fell fighting in Africa for Free France and democracy during World War II; 333 of these men have their last resting places in the cemetery's section H. Section B is devoted to children who died in infancy, and the oldest part, to the left of the obelisk as you come in, contains the tombs of colonists from the 1920s and 1930s, most of whom seem to have been less than forty years old when they died. The cemetery is nowadays also home to a colony of cats.

The palmery

Northeast of town, between the Route de Fes (N8) and the Route de Casablanca (N9). Marrakesh's **palmery** is dotted with the villas of prosperous Marrakshis, and also boasts a golf course and a couple of luxury hotels. The clumps of date palms look rather windswept, but the palmery does have a certain tranquillity, and it's several degrees cooler than the Medina, which makes it a particular attraction in summer. Supposedly, it sprang from stones spat out by the date-munching troops of Marrakesh's founder, Youssef Ben Tachfine, but there's no way this story can be true, as the dates produced by its fifty thousand-odd palms are not of eating quality, and are fit only for animal feed.

The most popular route through the oasis is the **Circuit de la Palmeraie**, which meanders through the trees and villas from the Route de Fes to the Route de Casablanca. The classic way to see it is by *calèche* (see p.132), and the Marrakech Tour sightseeing bus travels round it too. If you're in a walking mood, and fancy tackling the Circuit de la Palmeraie on foot (quite a long 5km stroll), you can get there by ordinary public transport, taking bus #17 or #26 to the Route de Fes turn-off, and bus #1 back

▲ CAMELS IN THE PALMERY

from the Route de Casablanca (or vice versa). It's also possible to ride around the palmery on a camel – men by the main road offer rides.

Shops, markets and galleries

Alimentation Générale

54 Av Mohammed V, at the corner of Rue Mohammed Bekal. Daily 8am–1pm & 2.30–8pm. Forget the groceries – they're just a front for what this place really sells, which is booze. You'll find a number of different spirits, some familiar, others less so (the stuff in what looks like a Ricard bottle is popular locally, but best avoided). Moroccan wines, mostly red, are notoriously variable; the top choice here is CB, at 140dh a bottle, followed by Medaillon (90dh) and Domaine de Sahari (65dh). Among the cheap brands (35dh), Cabernet and Ksar are usually quite drinkable.

Amazonite

94 Bd El Mansour Eddahbi, Guéliz ☎044 44 99 26. Mon–Sat 9am–1pm & 3.30–7.30pm. The Marrakesh branch of a Casablanca shop long known for its fine stock of *objets d'art*, Amazonite is the product of the owner's passion for rare and beautiful things. Most of the pieces are antique, with a hefty proportion comprised of jewellery; if asked, staff explain each item with charm and grace.

Aswak Assalam

Av 11 Janvier at the junction with Av Prince Moulay Abdallah, Guéliz. Daily 7am–9.30pm. A hypermarket, and certainly not the most characterful shopping in town, but quick and easy for certain things. There's a good patisserie section, and serve-yourself grains and spices, so you can weigh out exactly as much or as little as you want. You'll also find a fuller (and probably fresher) range of commercial dairy products than you would at a grocery store, and there are even consumer items like TVs and kitchenware, including couscous steamers.

Bazar Atlas

129 Av Mohammed V, Guéliz ☎063 62 01 03. Daily 7am–9.30pm. Some exquisite and interesting items grace this elegant little shop, mostly silver jewellery, but also ornaments for the home, including inkpots made from ram's horns, and colonial-era glass boxes. The selection is not huge, but it's well chosen.

La Galerie Bleue

119 Av Mohammed V, Guéliz ℡044
42 00 80. Daily 10am–1pm & 4–8pm.
The chicest of Marrakesh's
art galleries, which specializes
in modern paintings from
Morocco and abroad, most in
striking colours. The selection
concentrates on abstract paintings
– though not exclusively – and
there are also a few sculptures.

Librairie Chatr

19 Av Mohammed V, Guéliz ℡044
44 79 97. Mon–Sat 8am–1pm &
3–8pm. This bookshop and
stationer's sells mainly French
titles, but there's also a shelf
of English-language titles,
mostly classics, at the back on
the right. The front part of the
shop supplies artists' materials,
including paint and brushes,
as well as a large and varied
selection of pens.

Librairie d'Art ACR

Résidence Tayeb, 55 Bd Mohammed
Zerktouni, Guéliz ℡044 44 67 92.
Mon–Sat 9am–12.30pm & 3–7pm.
This bookshop stocks the
beautiful ACR range of French
art and coffee-table books,
including several on Marrakesh
and Moroccan interior design.
There are also books on subjects
such as architecture, textiles and
jewellery.

L'Orientaliste

11 & 15 Rue de la Liberté, Guéliz
℡044 43 40 74. Mon–Sat
9am–12.30pm & 3–7.30pm, Sun
9am–12.30pm. Specializing in
rather chic North African-style
home furnishings, L'Orientaliste
also does a fine line in limited
Moroccan pop-art screen-prints
by local artist Hassan Hajjaj. At
no. 15 it's mainly furniture that's
stocked, while at no. 11 they
concentrate on smaller items,
including glassware and perfume.

Lun'art Gallery

24 Rue Moulay Ali, Guéliz ℡044 44
72 66. Mon–Sat 9.30am–12.30pm &
4–8pm. Despite its name, this is
really an interior design shop,
with a selection of furniture and
accessories for the home, both
old and new. Nonetheless, it's
the paintings that most inspire
– modern, lively and full of
strong Moroccan characters.

Marché Central (Municipal Market)

Rue Ibn Toumert. Mon–Sat 7am–8pm,
Sun 7am–1pm, though shops within
the market may keep shorter hours.
A far cry from the markets in
the Medina, and much more
like those of Continental
Europe, this is where expats
and better-off Marrakshis come
for their fresh fish, meat, fruit
and veg. There are also cut
flowers, souvenir stalls selling
pottery, fossils and tourist tat,
and two butchers specializing
in horsemeat. One shop of
particular interest is *Savonnerie
Artesanale*, on the outside of the
building (Mon–Sat 9am–2pm
& 4–7pm), which sells natural

▼ PETIT TAXI STAND

palm oil based soaps with a range of ingredients added for fragrance and health – green tea, coffee, argan oil and cinnamon.

Nouvelle Galerie d'Antiquités

72 Av Mohammed V, Guéliz ☎ 044 44 98 60. Mon–Sat 10am–1pm & 3.30–7.30pm. Kitsch, but old kitsch, with lots of colonial-era brass statuary, samovars, chandeliers, carriage clocks and crockery, plus a cabinet full of old books and manuscripts (mostly Arabic). It's expensive, but worth a browse if you like antiques.

Place Vendôme

141 Av Mohammed V, Guéliz ☎ 044 43 52 63. Mon–Sat 9am–12.30pm & 3–7.30pm, Sun 9am–12.30pm. Moroccan leather is world famous, and you'll certainly find it here, along with some very sumptuous soft leather and suede, in the form of bags, belts, wallets and clothes. Purses start at 100dh, and there are some very stylish ladies' garments – jackets, coats and dresses – at around 3000dh.

Cafés and patisseries

Amandine

177 Rue Mohammed el Bekal. Daily 7am–1pm & 4–9pm. If you're on a diet, look away now, because this is a double whammy: a café-patisserie, stuffed full of the most scrumptious almond-filled Moroccan pastries and French-style cream cakes you could imagine, and right next door, a plush ice-cream parlour where you can sit and eat in comfort. You can have a coffee with your choice of sweetmeat in both halves, but the ice-cream section is more spacious, while the patisserie concentrates on the takeaway trade.

Boule de Neige

20 Rue de Yougoslavie, just off Place Abdelmoumen Ben Ali. Daily 7am–10pm. This lively patisserie serves Continental and American breakfasts and all-day snacks, as well as good ice cream and coffee. It also serves toast with *amalou* – a tasty paste made of honey, almonds and the exquisite, nutty oil of the argan tree, found only in the south of Morocco. On Saturday and Sunday evenings, there's live Moroccan pop music too.

Café des Negotiants

Place Abdelmoumen Ben Ali. Daily 6am–midnight. Slap bang on the busiest corner in Guéliz, this grand café is the place to sit out on the pavement and really feel that you're in the heart of modern Marrakesh. It's also an excellent venue in which to spend the morning over a coffee, with a choice of different croissants (plain, chocolate, almond), or even crepes and fruit juice, to accompany your caffeine fix.

▼ SOLARIS

Café la Siroqua

20 Bd Mohammed Zerktouni, next to the Colisée cinema. Daily 5am–10pm. Near the CTM bus depot, this café is a favourite spot for breakfast, serving croissants, orange juice and coffee. There's a choice of seats: out on the pavement, or in an a/c salon with tinted windows.

Oliveri

Av el Mansour Eddahbi, behind Hotel Agdal. Daily 6.30am–10pm. The Marrakesh branch of a Casablanca firm that's been serving delicious, creamy, Italian-style ices since colonial times, this is the poshest ice-cream parlour in town. You can eat your scoop from a proper ice-cream goblet among elegant surroundings, accompanied, should you so desire, by coffee; or else you can take it away in a waffle cone.

Solaris

170 Av Mohammed V. Daily 5am–10pm. This bright establishment under a neon sign looks just a tad more modern and sophisticated than your average Marrakesh coffee house, with tiled floors and mirror panels behind the bar. The wicker chairs and tables are just right to relax at with your coffee and croissant while you watch the comings and goings along the boulevard.

Restaurants

Al Fassia

Résidence Tayeb, 55 Bd Mohammed Zerktouni, Guéliz ☎044 43 40 60. Daily noon–2.30pm & 7.30–11pm. Truly Moroccan – both in decor and cuisine – and specializing in dishes from the country's culinary capital, Fes. Start with that great classic, pigeon pastilla, followed by a choice of four different lamb tajines, among other fine Fassi offerings. There's a lunchtime set menu for around 150dh, but dinner will cost twice that. The ambience and service are superb.

Bagatelle

101 Rue Yougoslavie ☎044 44 02 74. Daily except Wed noon–2.30pm & 7.30–10.30pm. Photos of Marrakesh in the 1950s deck the walls, and there's a lovely vine-shaded garden to eat in at this French-style restaurant which first opened its doors in 1949. You can start with an entrée such as pork and guinea fowl terrine, or pan-fried lamb's brain with capers, take in some Portuguese-style veal tongue, or duck confit with baked apple for your main course, and finish off with tart of the day or lemon and vodka sorbet. Throw in a coffee or a mint tea, and you'll pay around 200–250dh per head.

Chez Jack'Line

63 Av Mohammed V, near Place Abdelmoumen Ben Ali ☎044 44 75 47. Daily noon–2.30pm & 7–11pm. French, Italian and Moroccan dishes are all served here under the skilful direction of the indefatigable Jack'Line Pinguet and the beady eye (upstairs) of Ulysses, her parrot. You can eat splendidly for 150dh à la carte, plus wine – top choices are the steaks and pasta dishes, including superb cannelloni – or go for the good-value 80dh set menu based on couscous or tajine.

Chez Pierre

Rue Oum Rabia, next to the Diamant Noir nightclub. Daily 24hr. Sandwiches, omelettes, crepes and pizzas, all served round

M.KAMAL

▲ FINE DINING IN THE VILLE NOUVELLE

the clock – very handy if you emerge from a night's clubbing with a ravenous hunger. The walls are decorated with 1960s black-and-white stills featuring personalities of the era from Brigitte Bardot to Jimi Hendrix, but it's the hours rather than the decor which most appeal.

Grand Café de la Poste

Rue el Imam Malik, just off Av Mohammed V behind the post office ☎ 044 43 30 38. Daily 8am–1am. More grand than café, this is in fact quite a posh restaurant serving modern international cuisine (roast chicken with vanilla mashed potatoes, for example). Main courses go for 100–150dh. There's even Earl Grey tea to wash it down; alternatively you can have mint tea or coffee, or a choice of rums, tequilas and fine brandies if you prefer something harder.

Hotel Farouk

66 Av Hassan II ☎ 044 43 19 89. Daily 5am–10pm. From noon the hotel restaurant offers an excellent-value 50dh set menu with soup, salad, couscous, tajine or brochettes, followed by fruit, ice cream or home-made yoghurt. Alternatively, tuck in to one of their excellent wood-oven pizzas.

La Taverne

22 Bd Mohammed Zerktouni ☎ 044 44 61 26. Daily 12.30–3pm & 7–10.30pm. As well as a drinking tavern, this is a pretty decent restaurant – in fact, it claims to be the oldest in town – where you can dine on French and Moroccan fare indoors or in a lovely tree-shaded garden. The 110dh four-course set menu is great value.

La Trattoria

179 Rue Mohammed el Bekal ☎ 024 43 26 41, ⊛ www.latrattoriamarrakech .com. Daily 7–11.30pm. The best Italian food in town, with impeccable, friendly service and excellent cooking. The restaurant is located in a 1920s house decorated by the acclaimed American designer Bill Willis. As well as freshly made pasta, steaks and escalopes, there are specialities like *tagliata de boeuf* – made with beef, capers and herbs from the Atlas mountains – plus a wonderful tiramisú to squeeze in for afters.

Le Cantanzaro

50 Rue Tarik Ibn Ziad ☎ 044 43 37 31. Mon–Sat noon–2.30pm & 7.30–11.30pm. Behind the municipal market, near the *Hôtel Toulousain*, this is one of the city's most popular Italian restaurants,

crowded at lunchtime with Marrakshis, expats and tourists. Specialities include *saltimbocca alla romana* and rabbit in mustard sauce, and there's *crème brûlée* or tiramisú to round it off with. You're strongly advised to book, but you can also just turn up and queue for a table.

Le Jacaranda

32 Bd Mohammed Zerktouni ☎044 44 72 15, ⊛www.lejacaranda.ma. Daily noon–2.45pm & 7.30–11pm. Reliable French and Moroccan cuisine, starting with the likes of locally renowned oysters from Oualidia on the coast, beef carpaccio, or snails in garlic butter, followed by duck confit with baked apples and wild mushrooms, or perhaps just a bream tajine. À la carte eating will set you back around 300dh a head plus wine, or there's a lunchtime set menu for 105dh. The restaurant doubles as an art gallery, with different exhibits on its walls each month.

Lunch d'Or

Rue de l'Imam Ali. Daily 12.30–10pm. It can be hard to find an honest-to-goodness cheap Moroccan eatery in the Ville Nouvelle, but this place is one of a pair opposite the church

serving tasty tajines at 20dh a shot, as well as salads, brochettes and pizzas; great value and very popular with workers on their lunch break.

Paradise des Îles

Rue Oum Rabia, on a side road off Av Mohammed V (look for the Pizza Hut on the opposite side of the avenue) ☎044 44 82 10. Mon–Sat noon–3pm & 7pm–midnight. The cuisine here is supposedly from the French Indian Ocean island of Réunion, and one or two dishes do indeed hail from there, notably the swordfish creole. In truth, however, the menu finds inspiration from a number of places, France and Morocco being, predictably, top of the list. Whatever the genre, the food's very tasty and there's a good-value 115dh lunchtime menu.

Restaurant 33 Marrakech

33 Av Mohammed V. Daily noon–3pm & 7pm–midnight. Quite smart for a mid-range place, with royal blue table cloths, and the usual favourites – tajine, couscous and tanjia – on the menu, along with a big choice of brochettes – lamb, veal, chicken, turkey, fish, kefta (minced lamb) and spicy merguez sausage. Wine is served, and there's a good-value 80dh menu.

▼ PARADISE NIGHTCLUB

▲ TERRACE AT THE CHESTERFIELD PUB

Restaurant Puerto Banus

Rue Ibn Hanbal, opposite the Police Headquarters and Royal Tennis Club ☎044 44 65 34, ⓦwww.restaurant -puertobanus.com. Daily noon–3pm & 7.30pm–midnight. A Spanish fish restaurant – though French-managed – with specialities such as gazpacho and paella, and oysters introduced from Japan to Oualidia on the Moroccan coast. There's also a good selection of French and Moroccan dishes, including seafood pastilla. Count on 200dh per head without wine à la carte, though at lunchtimes there's a 95dh buffet.

Rôtisserie de la Paix

68 Rue de Yougoslavie, alongside the former cinema Lux-Palace ☎044 43 31 18, ⓦwww.restaurant-diaffa .ma. Daily noon–3pm & 7–11pm. An open-air grill, established in 1949, specializing in mixed grills barbecued over wood, usually with a fish option for non-meat-eaters. It's all served either in a salon with a roaring fire in winter, or in the shaded garden in summer. On Fridays, you can also go for the fish couscous.

The Red House

Boulevard el Yarmouk, opposite the Medina wall, Hivernage ☎044 43 70 40 or 41, ⓦwww.theredhouse -marrakech.com. Daily noon–2.30pm & 7.30–10.30pm. You'll need to reserve ahead to eat at this palatial riad, beautifully decorated in stucco and *zellij*. There's a Moroccan set menu (500dh), featuring pigeon pastilla, and lamb tajine with prunes and sesame, or you can dine à la carte on the likes of prawn and langouste ravioli or sashimi of trout and John Dory.

Bars

Café Atlas

Place Abdelmoumen Ben Ali. Daily 7am–11pm. A pavement café in the very centre of Guéliz, but wander inside, and hey presto, it is magically transformed into a bar, with bottled beer, spirits and plates of bar snacks on the counter. In theory, you could take your drink out on the pavement, but that would be considered rather indiscreet, so it's best to remain within, so where respectable passers-by won't notice that you're indulging in alcohol.

Café-Bar de l'Escale

Rue Mauritanie, just off Av Mohammed V. Daily 11am–11pm. An old-school all-male Moroccan drinking den which has been going since 1947. It's known for good bar snacks, such as fried fish or merguez sausages – you could even come here for lunch or dinner (there's a dining area at the back). Not recommended for unaccompanied women.

Chesterfield Pub

Gallerie Merchande, 119 Av Mohammed V. Daily 10am–midnight. Next to the *Nassim Hotel*, this supposedly English pub – it's nothing of the sort – is one of Marrakesh's more sophisticated watering holes, with a cosy if rather smoky bar area, all soft seats and muted lighting. There's also a more relaxed, open-air poolside terrace to lounge about on with your draught beer or cocktail of a summer evening.

Hotel Agdal

1 Bd Mohammed Zerktouni. Daily 7pm–midnight. The bar here is pretty peaceful as Moroccan drinking holes go, and one where women should feel reasonably comfortable despite the presence of a few prostitutes. You can sit at the bar or more discreetly at one of the tables.

Samovar

145 Rue Mohammed el Bekal, Guéliz, next to the Hôtel Oudaya. Daily 10am–11pm. Samovar is an old-school, low-life drinking den; a male hangout with bar girls in attendance. The customers get more and more out of it as the evening progresses – if you want to see the underbelly of Morocco's drinking culture, this is the place. Definitely not recommended for women visitors, however.

Nightclubs

Diamant Noir

Rue Oum er Bia, behind Hôtel Marrakesh, Guéliz ☎044 43 43 51.

Daily 11pm–3am. Entry 80dh–100dh includes one drink. Look for the signpost on Av Mohammed V to find this lively dance club where Western pop and disco alternate with Algerian and Moroccan *raï* music – it's the latter that really fills the dance floor. There are two bars, quite a sophisticated range of drinks, and a mainly young crowd – a mixture of couples, singles and a gay contingent.

New Feeling

Hotel Palmeraie Golf Palace, Palmery ☎044 30 10 10. Daily 11pm–4am. Entry 200dh A bit of a haul from town, unless you're staying at the hotel of course, but very popular with Marrakesh's bright young things (even the king was known to frequent it in his youth), this glitzy discotheque is the place to see and be seen, to hang out and be elegant, and maybe even have a little turn on the dancefloor. Dress to impress if you want to get in.

Pacha Marrakech

Av Mohammed VI (southern extension), Nouvelle Zone Hôtelière de l'Aguedal ☎044 38 84 00, ⊛www.pachamarrakech.com. Daily midnight–5am. Sun–Thurs 100–150dh; Fri & Sat: 200–250dh; occasionally as much as 350dh for a big event; entry includes one

▼ DIAMANT NOIR

▲ PACHA MARRAKECH

drink. The Marrakesh branch of the famous Ibiza club, now an international chain, claims to have the biggest and best sound system in Africa, and it's certainly the place to come if DJing skills, acoustics and visuals are important for your clubbing experience. Big-name DJs from abroad regularly play here – check the website for current line-ups. There's even a free shuttle service to and from town (call to arrange).

Paradise Disco

Hotel Mansour Eddahbi, Bd El Mansour Eddahbi, Hivernage ☎044 33 91 00. Daily midnight–4am. Entry 150dh weekdays, 200dh weekends. A plush and trendy club that tries to be reasonably exclusive (so dress smartly). The clientele of well-heeled Moroccans, with a sprinkling of expats, plus a few tourists staying at the attached five-star hotel, dance to some well-mixed sounds, mostly at the commercial – or at least, the more tuneful – end of house and techno. The drinks list is impressively long, and impressively expensive.

Point Rouge

68 Bd Zerktouni, Guéliz. Daily 11pm–3am. Entry 50dh includes one drink. This is not the poshest joint in town – in fact it's a bit of a dive – but it's got to be the most good-natured and the least pretentious place for a dance. Drunken bonhomie reigns as a mixed crowd of all ages do their thing to the sound of a four-piece Arabic folk band with female vocalist, interspersed with disco, pop and even hip-hop records. No one stands on ceremony and a good time is generally had by all.

VIP Club

Place de la Liberté, Guéliz. Daily midnight–4am. Entrance 100dh weekdays, 150dh weekends. The gullet-like entrance leads down to the first level, where there's an "oriental cabaret" (meaning a belly-dancing floor show), and then further down to the deepest level, where there's what the French call a *boîte*, meaning a sweaty little nightclub. It's got a circular dancefloor and a small bar area, but despite its diminutive size, the place rarely seems to be full.

Atlas excursions

The countryside around Marrakesh is some of the most beautiful in Morocco. The High Atlas mountains that make such a spectacular backdrop to the city are even more impressive when you're actually among them. For a spot of hiking, or even skiing, they're easy enough to reach in an hour or two by grand taxi (see p.131) from the gare routière de Bab er Robb, 2km southwest of the Jemaa el Fna. Imlil is the best base for mountain treks, but Setti Fatma, in the beautiful Ourika Valley, is more picturesque, and handier for less strenuous walking, while Oukaïmeden is Morocco's premier ski resort.

Imlil

You can take in the village of **IMLIL** on a day-trip out of Marrakesh, but it's more worthwhile if you spend a night or two there and do a bit of walking in the surrounding countryside (for hiking suggestions, see p.101). To reach Imlil by public transport, get a shared *grand taxi* from Bab er Robb *gare routière* to **ASNI** (1hr), where there are *grands taxis* on to Imlil (30min). Each leg of the journey should cost 15dh per person. Alternatively, you could charter a *grand taxi*

to take you up there from Marrakesh. This should work out at around 400dh for the round trip, including three or four hours' waiting time.

The mule trail back down to Asni is a relatively easy six-hour **hike** from Imlil, and there are vehicles from Asni back to Marrakesh until around 5pm. Alternatively, you could just have **lunch** in Imlil and then head back into town by taxi. An excellent place to eat is the British-run *Kasbah du Toubkal* (see p.56), which has a 300dh set menu. This should

▼ SNAKE CHARMER AT WATERFALL, ATLAS MOUNTAINS

be booked at least a day in advance, and in fact the *Kasbah* can organize the whole day-trip from Marrakesh as a package should you so desire, at 850dh per person (to arrange it, call ☎044 48 56 11). At the very least, it's worth popping into the *Kasbah* for a mint tea on their scenic terrace. Other places in the village offer a cheaper lunch, including the *Café du Soleil* by the taxi stand, and the *Café les Amis*, 200m up the road, which can lay on a tajine for one, two or more people if you order it at least an hour and a half in advance.

The Ourika Valley

More picturesque than Imlil, and more worthwhile for a day trip, is the village of **SETTI FATMA**, at the top of the highly scenic **Ourika Valley**, which starts around 40km out of Marrakesh. Setti Fatma is served by regular *grands taxis* from Bab er Robb *gare routière*, taking around an hour to reach

▼ ATLAS MOUNTAIN VILLAGE

Setti Fatma Moussem

Every year in mid-August, Setti Fatma holds a **moussem** dedicated to the local saint after whom the village is named. The saint's tomb stands by the river on the way to the waterfalls above the village. Although the *moussem* is religious in origin, it is just as much a fair and market, attracting Sufi mystics as well as performers like those of Marrakesh's Jemaa el Fna. All in all it's an enjoyable family occasion, with adults and children from the village and the surrounding area taking part.

and costing 25dh per person. If you charter a whole taxi (300dh for the round trip plus waiting time), you'll be able to stop off wherever you like en route to enjoy the scenery, take photographs and buy souvenirs, including locally found fossils of ammonites and trilobites – sea animals which became extinct around 42 million years ago.

Setti Fatma is an excellent base for scenic **walks**, with six (sometimes seven) waterfalls above the village, the first of which can be reached very easily; you'll have no shortage of would-be guides offering to show you the way for a tip (of course), best agreed in advance.

There are plenty of good spots to stop for a bite to **eat** in Setti Fatma, including the *Restaurant le Noyer* (daily 8am–6pm), which does tasty tajines, brochettes and salads, and the *Belle Rose* (daily 8am–4pm), which has a little terrace overlooking the river and is a great place to stop for a mint tea with 70dh set menus also available. Among the hotels (see p.126), the *Asgaour* serves good 50dh tajines, while the *Perle d'Ourika* and the *Sitti Fadma* both offer more scenic outdoor eating, with set menus at 80dh and 70dh respectively. For something a bit posher, *Auberge Ramuntcho*, 10km back down the valley and 4km above the village of Aghbalou (☎044 42 82 63), does set menus for 300dh.

Skiing in Oukaïmeden

Morocco may not strike you as a country to go skiing in, but the High Atlas village of **OUKAÏMEDEN** ("Ouka" for short), 74km from Marrakesh, has 20km of runs to suit skiers and snowboarders at all levels. One of the ski lifts here was once the highest in the world, reaching 3273m. It's now supplemented by four shorter lifts, and it is possible to reach even higher terrain using donkeys – an option you don't get at Aspen or St Moritz. There are nursery and intermediate runs on the lower slopes for the less advanced, and off-piste skiing and snowboarding are also available.

Snowfall and snow cover are variable, with **conditions** generally at their best in late January and early February. The slopes are sometimes icy early in the morning and wet by afternoon, and pistes are not tremendously well cared for (beware of hidden rocks), but not having to queue in the mornings lets you get in plenty of skiing.

In winter, *grands taxis* serve Oukaïmeden from Marrakesh. You have to pay for the round trip (100dh), even if you intend to stay the night, and if not, you have to come back with the same taxi you took on the way up – the driver will tell you when he intends to return (usually 3pm or 4pm), and you have to turn up then or

▲ HIKING IN THE ATLAS MOUNTAINS

find some other way back to Marrakesh. Chartering a taxi costs 600dh there and back. A snowplough keeps access roads open in the skiing season (December to April inclusive), after which the ski lifts close, even if conditions are still good.

Ski lift passes cost just 50dh for a day, and lessons are available from local instructors. You can rent **equipment** from shops near the hotel *Chez Juju* (see p.126) and at the bottom of the slope for around 150dh a day (slightly more for snowboards); toboggans are also available.

Trekking and hiking in the Atlas

You could spend many days trekking in the High Atlas, but there are also trails to suit the casual hiker and routes that can be covered in a day. The easiest walks take in pretty valleys spread with a patchwork of little fields dotted with walnut trees. With the right equipment, clothing and supplies, it's even possible to climb **Jebel Toubkal** (4167m), North Africa's highest peak, though this is not an

ascent to be taken lightly. The best base for Jebel Toubkal is Imlil, from where the climb would take two to three days there and back.

A short trek from Imlil (see p.99) is the route to **Tachdirt** (3–4hr), which has a *CAF Refuge* where you can spend the night. From Tachdirt, it's a day's trek down to **Setti Fatma** (see p.100), where there's transport back to Marrakesh. Another option from Tachdirt is the superb day's walk to **Timichi**, where you can stay at a *gîte d'étape* – a private house where there are rooms for rent (expect to pay 30–50dh per person), then on the following day take a six-hour walk down to Setti Fatma, or across to Oukaïmeden (see p.101), or a seven- to nine-hour route down to Asni.

To hire a **guide**, (expect to pay 200–300dh per day), there are offices (called *Bureau de Guides et Accompagnateurs en Montagne*) in both Imlil (☎044 48 56 26) and Setti Fatma (☎073 26 73 93). In Marrakesh, the *Hotel Ali* (see p.115) is one of the best places to get information and arrange guides.

Essaouira

Around 170km west of Marrakesh, the seaside resort of Essaouira has had a special relationship with tourists since the 1960s, when its popularity as a hippy resort attracted the likes of Jimi Hendrix and Frank Zappa. Since then it has become a centre for artists and windsurfers, but despite increasing numbers of foreign visitors it remains one of the most laid-back and likeable towns in Morocco. The whitewashed and blue-shuttered houses of its Medina, enclosed by spectacular ramparts, provide a colourful backdrop to a long, sandy beach.

The Medina

The fairy-tale **ramparts** around Essaouira's Medina may look medieval, but they actually date from the reign of eighteenth-century sultan Sidi Mohammed Ben Abdallah, who commissioned a French military architect named Theodore Cornut to build a new town on a site previously occupied by a series of forts. The result is a walled Medina with a unique blend of Moroccan and French street layouts, combining a crisscross of main streets with a labyrinth of alleyways between them.

At the heart of the Medina are the main **souks**, centred on two arcades either side of Rue Mohammed Zerktouni. On the northwest side is the **spice souk**, where culinary aromatics join incense, traditional cosmetics and even natural aphrodisiacs billed as "herbal Viagra". Across the way, the **jewellers' souk** sells not just gems but also all kinds of crafts.

The western part of the Medina, the **Kasbah**, centres on **Place Prince Moulay el Hassan**. This is the town's main square, where locals and tourists alike linger over a mint tea or a coffee and enjoy the lazy pace of life. The square to the south, the **Mechouar**, is bounded by an imposing wall topped by a clocktower and flanked by palm trees, in whose shade townspeople often take a breather from the heat of the day.

The Skala de la Ville

Rue de Skala. Daily sunrise–sunset. Free. The city's northern bastion, the **Skala de la Ville**, commands panoramic views across the Medina and out to sea.

▼ MEDINA, ESSAOUIRA

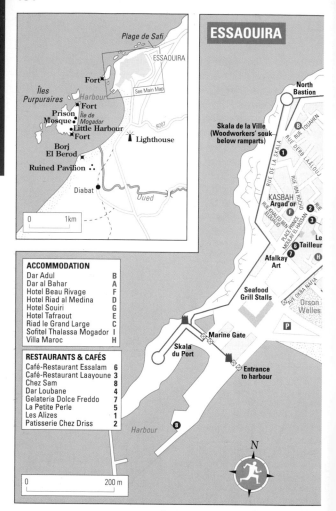

ESSAOUIRA

ACCOMMODATION

Dar Adul	B
Dar al Bahar	A
Hotel Beau Rivage	F
Hotel Riad al Medina	D
Hotel Souiri	G
Hotel Tafraout	E
Riad le Grand Large	C
Sofitel Thalassa Mogador	I
Villa Maroc	H

RESTAURANTS & CAFÉS

Café-Restaurant Essalam	6
Café-Restaurant Laayoune	3
Chez Sam	8
Dar Loubane	4
Gelateria Dolce Freddo	7
La Petite Perle	5
Les Alizes	1
Patisserie Chez Driss	2

Getting to Essaouira

Reaching Essaouira from Marrakesh by public transport is a cinch, though the journey time means you'll probably want to stay overnight. The cheapest way is to get a **bus** (15 daily; 3hr 30min; around 35dh) from the *gare routière* (see p.138). You arrive at Essaouira's bus station, a ten-minute walk outside Essaouira's Bab Doukkala, or a short *petit taxi* ride from the Medina (5dh). A faster and more comfortable bus service is provided by **Supratours** (3 daily; 2hr 30min; 60dh), leaving from Marrakesh's train station and arriving at Bab Marrakesh in Essaouira. At the time of writing, departures from Marrakesh were at 11am, 3.15pm and 7pm. It's usually no problem to get seats on Supratours services, though bear in mind that when they are busy (before and after

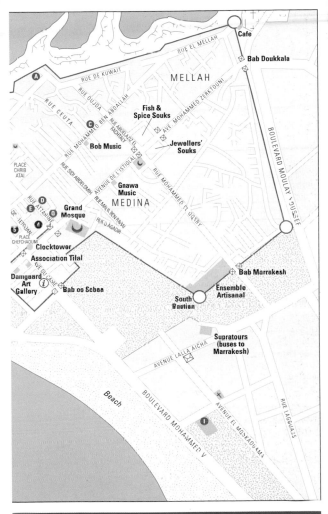

Eid el Kebir, and during the Gnaoua Music Festival at the end of June for example), priority is given to train passengers requiring an onward connection. CTM, the state bus company, also run a single daily service to Essaouira from their office on Boulevard Mohammed Zerktouni in Guéliz, currently departing at 8.30am, and arriving around 11am (60dh). Finally, there are shared **grands taxis** to Essaouira (2hr 30min; 70dh) from the rank behind Marrakesh's *gare routière*; in Essaouira they might drop you in town itself, though they actually operate from a yard by the bus station.

Essaouira's **tourist office** is located on Avenue du Caire (Mon–Fri 9am–6.30pm; ☏044 78 35 32).

The Gnaoua Festival

Essaouira's main annual event is the Gnaoua and World Music Festival (🌐 www
.festival-gnaoua.co.ma), usually held on the last weekend in June. The festival
focuses chiefly on the music of the **Gnaoua**, a Moroccan Sufi brotherhood with
West African roots going back to the days of slavery. Stages are set up in the plaza
between Place Prince Moulay el Hassan and the port, and outside Bab Marrakesh,
and performers come from Tangier, Marrakesh and, of course, Essaouira, with
special guests from Europe, the Caribbean and West Africa, in particular Senegal.
During the festival, which attracts as many as 200,000 people, you can expect
hotels and transport to be full, so book well ahead if possible.

It was one of the main Essaouira
locations used in Orson Welles's
1952 screen version of *Othello*.
Along the top are a collection of
European **cannons**, presented to
Sidi Mohammed Ben Abdallah
by ambitious nineteenth-century
merchants.

Down below, built into the
ramparts along the Rue de
Skala, you can see some of the
town's many **marquetry** and
woodcarving workshops, where
artisans produce amazingly
painstaking and beautiful pieces
from **thuya** wood.

The Skala du Port

Daily 8.30am–noon & 2.30–6pm. 10dh.
The **Skala du Port**, the square
sea bastion by the harbour,

topped by lookout posts in each
of its four corners, is worth
popping into for the **views**
from the ramparts. Looking east,
you have a brilliant vista along
the seaward side of the walled
city, especially pretty towards
sunset, when it's often bathed
in a pinkish glow. To the south,
the Skala overlooks the bustling
port area, where local wooden
fishing boats are built or
repaired, and where the fishing
fleet brings in the day's catch.

The beach

The main **beach**, to the south
of town, extends for miles.
On its early reaches, the chief
activity is **football** – a game is
virtually always in progress, and

▼ CANNONS ON THE SKALA DE LA VILLE

▲ BEACH, ESSAOUIRA

at weekends there's a full-scale local league.

The wind here can be a bit remorseless for sunbathing in spring and summer, but it's perfect for **windsurfing**, and Essaouira is Morocco's number one windsurfing resort. Equipment can be rented on the beach at Magic Fun Afrika (☎061 10 37 77, ✉magicfunafrika@hotmail .com; closed Dec–Feb), 500m south of the Medina, or a little further down the beach at Club Mistral (☎044 78 39 34, ✉morocco@club-mistral .com), open most of the year, but sometimes closed in January. The Royal Windsurfing Club (*Royal Club de Planche à Voile*), next to Magic Fun Afrika, offers windsurfing lessons. The water is cool enough to make a wetsuit essential year-round.

If you head further along the beach, past the football and the crowds, you'll pass the riverbed of the Oued Ksob (which can't be crossed at high tide) and come upon the ruins of an eighteenth-century circular fort, the **Borj el Berod**, which looks as though it is almost melting into the sand. Local legend has it that Jimi Hendrix played impromptu concerts here for his fellow hippies, but the story that it inspired his "Castles Made of Sand" is definitely apocryphal, as the track was recorded long before he came to town.

Shops and galleries

Afalkay Art

9 Place Prince Moulay el Hassan ☎044 47 60 89. Daily 9am–8pm. A vast emporium of thuya marquetry and woodcarving, with a massive selection of boxes, chess and backgammon sets, furniture, sculptures and carvings (some of which are from Senegal rather than local). It also has marked, fixed prices, so it's a good place to see what's available and how much it's going to cost, even if you end up doing your shopping elsewhere.

Argad'or

5 Rue Ibn Rochd ☎044 78 40 69. Daily 10am–9pm. The argan tree, which grows only in the south of Morocco, produces an exquisite and much prized nutty oil which is great in leaf and nut salads, drizzled over lamb-and-prune tajines, or mixed with almond butter to make a delicious paste called *amalou*. Lately, argan oil is also being marketed as a

▲ SKALA DU PORT

cosmetic, either rubbed onto your skin as is, or mixed into various creams and unguents. This shop sells everything from the oil itself (from 230dh a litre) to argan honey, *amalou* and assorted argan-derived cosmetics, even argan-based suntan oil (what a waste).

Association Tillal des Arts Plastiques

4 Rue du Caire. Daily 8.30am–12.30pm & 2.30–7pm. Essaouira's cheap and cheerful art gallery, where you can pick up small works of art including colourful naive domestic scenes by Najia Kerairate, and humorous caricatures of Moroccan life by Hamid Bouhali, for as little as 100dh.

Bob Music

104 Av Sidi Mohammed Ben Abdallah. Daily 9am–8pm. An instrument shop selling several types of Moroccan drums, gnaoua castanets, lutes, *Ginbris* (an instrument not unlike a lute, but rather more rustic), and even the sort of pipes used by snake charmers. The shop is named after Bob Marley, though none of the instruments are actually used in Jamaican reggae music – the association of course is in the spirit, not the sound.

Galerie d'Art Frederic Damgaard

Av Oqba Ibn Nafia, Mechouar ☎044 78 44 46. Daily 9am–1pm & 3–7pm. Essaouira's artists have made a name for themselves in both Morocco and Europe. Those whose paintings and sculptures are exhibited here in Essaouira's top gallery have developed their own highly distinctive styles, in some cases attracting an entourage of imitators. The gallery was run by a Danish furniture designer, who also had an *atelier* at 2 Rue El Hijalli, just off Place Chefchaouni, but he has recently retired and at last check his place was up for sale; the good news however is that he will only sell it to someone who agrees to keep an art gallery.

Gnawa Music

60 Av de l'Istiqlal. Daily 10am–10pm. CDs (25dh) and cassettes (15dh) of North African and Muslim West African music – most especially music of the type played at the annual Gnaoua Festival (see p.106), of which a compilation album is released each year. There's also classical Moroccan, Arab-Andalusian, Moroccan folk and Algerian *raï*. Another shop a few doors down at no. 52 sells a selection

focusing more on *raï*, pop and foreign sounds.

Le Tailleur
1 Rue el Hajali. Daily 9am–8pm.
A tailor, as the name says, but one who makes light cotton and linen clothing, mostly in cream, white, black and grey; beautifully cool in Morocco's sometimes relentless heat. Shirts, drawstring trousers, dresses and kaftans start at 130dh. Two doors up at no. 5, another shop sells similar clothes, but sewn together from pieces of different cloths, making them a mite more funky (though most are still in the same shades).

Cafés and ice-cream parlours

Gelateria Dolce Freddo
On the plaza between Place Prince Moulay el Hassan and the port. Daily 8am–10pm. Delicious Italian ice creams at just 5dh a scoop – the tiramisú flavour is to die for; the hazelnut isn't bad either.

Patisserie Chez Driss
10 Rue Hajjali, just off Place Prince Moulay el Hassan. Daily 7am–6pm.
Well established as one of Essaouira's most popular meeting places, serving delicious fresh pastries and coffee in a quiet leafy courtyard. It's the ideal spot for a leisurely breakfast.

Restaurants

Café-Restaurant Essalam
23 Place Prince Moulay el Hassan. Daily 8am–3.30pm & 6–10pm.
Though the choice is a little bit limited at this popular budget eating place, they do have by far the cheapest set menus in town (28–40dh), as well as tajines and Continental breakfasts (10dh).

Café-Restaurant Laayoune
4 Rue Hajjali ☏ 044 47 46 43. Daily noon–3pm & 7–11pm. Good for moderately priced tajines and other Moroccan staples in a relaxed setting with friendly service, though you may find the low tables and divan seating a bit awkward. You can eat à la carte (main dishes around 50dh) or choose from a range of tajine- and couscous-based set menus (58–78dh).

Chez Sam
In the fishing port ☏ 044 47 62 13. Daily noon–3pm & 7–11pm.
An Essaouira institution – a wooden shack, built like a boat, set seductively right by the waterfront in the harbour. Service can be a bit hit-and-miss but the portions are generous, the fish is usually cooked pretty well, there's beer and wine and you can watch

▼ FISHERMAN, ESSAOUIRA

the fishing boats through the portholes. The best fish is only available à la carte (main dishes around 90–100dh); there's a good-value set menu for 85dh, or one with lobster for 220dh.

Dar Loubane

24 Rue du Rif, near Place Chefchaouni ☎044 47 62 96. Daily noon–2pm & 7–10pm. On the ground-floor patio of an attractive eighteenth-century mansion, this upmarket restaurant serves up fine Moroccan and French cuisine (main dishes around 90dh, lunchtime set menu 95dh) among an eccentric collection of interesting, sometimes rather kitsch odds and ends that decorate the walls and the courtyard. There's live Gnaoua music on Saturday evening, when it's advisable to make a booking.

La Petite Perle

2 Rue el Hajali ☎044 47 50 50. Daily noon–2pm & 7–10pm. Great value

▼ HOTEL RIAD MEDINA

and a charming ambience, with set menus of good Moroccan food at 65–95dh, though it's equally good value to eat à la carte. Their *tajine de calamars* (which we suspect is actually made with octopus rather than squid, though they won't admit to this) is wonderful, and they sometimes do an eel tajine (*tajine de congres*) as well. The only downside is the back-breakingly low tables, which are at almost the same height as the seats.

Les Alizes

26 Rue de la Skala ☎044 47 68 19. Daily noon–3pm & 7–10pm. This little place away from the mainstream has built itself quite a reputation for well-prepared traditional Moroccan dishes. Choice is limited to an 85dh set menu, but everything is absolutely delicious. Wine is available; booking advised.

Seafood grill stalls

Off Place Prince Moulay el Hassan, on the way to the port. Daily noon–10pm. An absolute must if you're staying in Essaouira is a meal at one of these makeshift grill stalls, with wooden tables and benches. Each displays a selection of freshly caught fish, prawns, squid, lobster and other seafood delights – all you need to do is check the price (haggling is *de rigueur*) and select the marine denizens of your choice, which are whisked off to the barbecue to reappear on your plate a few minutes later. Despite the initial hustle for custom, the atmosphere is relaxed and standards high. Expect to pay 30dh for a simple fish supper or 150dh for one featuring lobster or langouste.

Accommodation

Accommodation

Marrakesh has a good selection of accommodation in all price ranges. The big trend in town at the moment is the **riad** or *maison d'hôte*, of which there are now over four hundred and eighty in Marrakesh, mostly in the **Medina**. Originally, a riad meant a house built around a patio garden (in fact, the term correctly refers to the garden rather than the house); *maison d'hôte* is just French for "guest house".

The trend started in the 1990s, when Europeans who'd bought houses in the Medina for their own use discovered they could make a pretty penny by taking in paying guests. Since then, the whole thing has escalated into something of an industry (a bubble waiting to burst in the eyes of some), and it's spread to other Moroccan cities, most notably Fes and Essaouira.

From the owners' point of view, a riad is a canny investment, and a step up in chic-ness from the small deluxe "boutique hotels" that are currently hyped on the international travel scene. For Marrakshis, although riads are driving Medina house prices out of the locals' league, they are also bringing a big injection of cash into the local economy, and are therefore a positive development.

Riads range from plain and simple lodgings in a Moroccan family home to restored old mansions with classic decor. Most common are Moroccan houses which have been done up by European owners to look like something from an interior-design magazine, with swimming pools in the patio and Jacuzzis on the roof.

At their best, riads allow you to stay in comfort in a classic Moroccan house eating fine cuisine, with a level of intimacy and stylish decor that no hotel can match. However, riads are often more expensive than hotels of a similar standard, and many are seriously overpriced, so it pays to shop around and be choosy.

As for **hotels**, the modern three-, four- and five-star establishments are concentrated in **Guéliz** and **Hivernage**, the latter district home to the big international chains. However, the very poshest establishments, such as the *La Mamounia* and the

Seasons vary slightly from establishment to establishment, but in general, **high season** for Marrakesh accommodation means March–May plus September and October, as well as Christmas and New Year. The rates quoted here – which include **breakfast** unless otherwise stated – are for the **cheapest double room** in high season; the rest of the year, you can expect prices to be anything from ten to fifty percent cheaper. However, if you intend to visit over **Christmas/New Year** period, note that this represents an exceptional peak within high season, when rates at some hotels can be as much as fifty percent higher than in the rest of the high season. Most hotels fix their prices in dirhams, but some upmarket establishments fix them in euros – don't worry though, you'll be able to pay in local currency.

ACCOMMODATION

Jemaa el Fna and the Southern Medina

Maison Arabe, offering palatial style along with the usual de luxe facilities (air conditioning, a swimming pool and gourmet dining), are back in the **Medina**. This is also where you'll find the most characterful mid-range hotels, usually in refurbished houses with en-suite rooms priced at 300–500dh. The cheapest hotels are mostly in the Medina too, and often handily close to the Jemaa el Fna. They offer doubles for around 100dh a night and shared showers and toilets.

If you want to lodge in more tranquil surroundings, it's also worth considering hotels in **Semlalia**, at the northern end of the Ville Nouvelle or, better still, a place out in the **palmery** to the northeast.

All of the top-end hotels and riads, and in fact many of the mid-range places too, take **reservations** online or by email, and even some inexpensive hotels can be booked by email. It's worth booking ahead, especially if you want to stay at one of the mid-range Medina hotels. At certain times of year, most notably around Christmas and Easter, you'll need to have reserved some time in advance, even to stay at one of the cheap hotels.

Jemaa el Fna and the Southern Medina

See map on pp.116–117.

Casa Lalla 16 Derb Jemaa ☏061 08 37 13, ⓦwww.casalalla.com. Hidden away down a twisty-turny back alley, but not very far from the Jemaa el Fna, this modern, deluxe riad is owned and run by the much acclaimed Michelin-starred chef Richard Neat, who deals with the catering, and his wife Sophie, who is responsible for the interior design. The decor is smooth and minimalist, with tadelakt-walled bathrooms, an in-house hammam and a walled roof terrace with views of the Atlas. The food is, of course, sublime. Doubles start at €105.

Dar les Cigognes 108 Rue Bab Berrima ☏044 38 27 40, ℻044 38 47 67, ⓦwww.lescigognes.com. A luxury riad run by a Swiss-American couple in two converted Medina houses. It's done up in traditional fashion around the patio, but with modern decor in the rooms and suites. There's a library, a salon and a terrace where you can see storks nesting on the walls of the royal palace opposite (hence the name, which means "house of the storks"). All rooms are en suite; doubles start at 1700dh.

Hotel Aday 111 Derb Sidi Bouloukat ☏044 44 19 20. This small budget hotel is well kept, clean, friendly and pleasantly decorated, with doors and ceilings painted in traditional Marrakshi style. The rooms, grouped around a central patio, are small and only some have external windows.

▲ CASA LALLA

Shower facilities are shared, with hot water round the clock. Doubles 100dh; breakfast not included. Single rooms are half that, which makes them just about the cheapest in town.

Hotel Ali Rue Moulay Ismail ☎ 044 44 49 79, ℻ 044 44 05 22, ✉ hotelali@hotmail .com. A popular hotel with en-suite rooms, heated in winter and a/c in summer. The hotel is used as an assembly point for various groups heading to the High Atlas, so it's a good source of trekking (and other) information. However, they don't always do a very good job of keeping out hustlers, and at times the place has the air of a transport terminal. The hotel changes money, rents bicycles, has a cybercafé and expedition provisions shop, and can arrange car, minibus or 4x4 rental. There's also a good-value restaurant with all-you-can-eat buffet suppers (see p.57). The rooms vary a lot, so it's worth checking them out before deciding

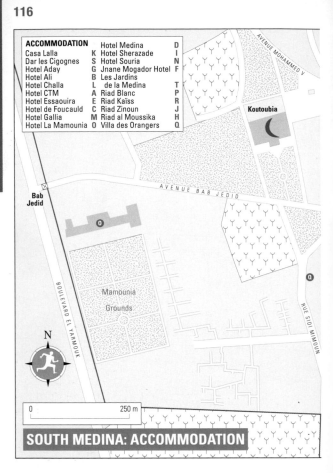

ACCOMMODATION		Hotel Medina	D
Casa Lalla	K	Hotel Sherazade	I
Dar les Cigognes	S	Hotel Souria	N
Hotel Aday	G	Jnane Mogador Hotel	F
Hotel Ali	B	Les Jardins	T
Hotel Challa	L	de la Medina	
Hotel CTM	A	Riad Blanc	P
Hotel Essaouira	E	Riad Kaïss	R
Hotel de Foucauld	C	Riad Zinoun	J
Hotel Gallia	M	Riad al Moussika	H
Hotel La Mamounia	O	Villa des Orangers	Q

SOUTH MEDINA: ACCOMMODATION

which to take. Book ahead, especially if you are likely to arrive late in the day. Doubles cost 250dh, dorm beds 60dh, the former including free use of the hotel's hammam.

Hotel Challa 14 Rue de la Recette ☎ & ☏044 44 29 77. A good-value budget hotel with nice, fresh rooms around a large formal patio with orange trees and a fountain. The bathroom facilities are shared (hot showers 10dh), and the roof terrace is nothing to write home about. Doubles 100dh excluding breakfast.

Hotel CTM Jemaa el Fna ☎044 44 23 25. This big old hotel has that much-sought-after quality: location, location,

location – above the former bus station on the Jemaa el Fna. The rooms are of a decent size, if drab, and some have their own shower. Rooms 28–32 overlook the Jemaa, which means that guests in those rooms can hear the performers day and night; the rooms at the back are much quieter. Breakfast is served on the roof terrace, which also overlooks the square. Doubles from 120dh.

Hotel Essaouira 3 Derb Sidi Bouloukat ☎ & ☏044 44 38 05. One of the most popular cheapies in Marrakesh – and with good reason. It's a well-run, safe place, with friendly management, and services

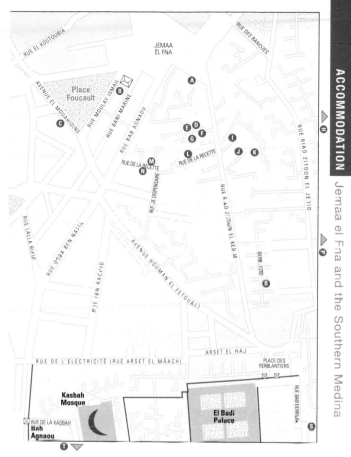

like laundry and a baggage deposit (handy if you're going trekking and don't want to carry all your luggage with you). Rooms are small and simple, and there's a rooftop café, where you can have breakfast. Reservations advised. Double rooms from 100dh excluding breakfast.

Hotel de Foucauld Av el Mouahidine
T044 44 08 06, F044 44 13 44. Rooms are on the small side but well kept and comfortable, with heating in winter, a/c in summer, and hot water round the clock. There's a roof terrace with views of the Koutoubia and the staff are friendly and helpful. Doubles 290dh.

Hotel Gallia 30 Rue de la Recette T044 44 59 13, F044 44 48 53, Wwww.ilove -marrakesh.com/hotelgallia. In a restored Medina mansion, this little gem is beautifully kept and spotlessly clean. The en-suite rooms are arranged around two tiled courtyards, one of which has a fountain and a palm tree with caged songbirds. There's central heating in winter and a/c in summer. Requires booking by fax, at least a month ahead if possible. Double rooms 450dh.

Hotel La Mamounia Av Bab Jedid T044 44 44 09, F044 44 49 40, Wwww.mamounia.com. Set within its own palatial grounds, this is Marrakesh's most famous hotel, and also its most expensive, with all the services you could want – a business centre, a fitness centre, tennis and squash courts, a beauty salon, its own hammam and sauna, a pool (of course), five restaurants, five bars and a casino. Decoratively, it is of most interest for the 1920s Art Deco touches by Jacques Majorelle (of Majorelle Garden fame), and their enhancements, in 1986, by the then Moroccan king's favourite designer, André Paccard. Despite the history, the fame and all the trimmings, standards of service here do not always match the price; *La Maison Arabe* (see p.120) is generally better value if you're looking to be pampered, though it can't match the *Mamounia*'s facilities or architectural splendour. Doubles from 3300dh; breakfast not included.

Hotel Medina 1 Derb Sidi Bouloukat ☎044 44 29 97. Located in a street full of good budget hotels, the *Medina* is a perennial favourite among the cheapies, and often full. It's clean, friendly and pretty good value, and the owner – who used to work in Britain as a circus acrobat – speaks good English. They have a small roof terrace where you can have breakfast; in summer there's also the option of sleeping on the roof (25dh). There's always hot water in the shared showers (5dh). Double rooms 100dh excluding breakfast (15dh).

Hotel Sherazade 3 Derb Djama, off Rue Riad Zitoun el Kadim ☎ & ℻044 42 93 05, ⓦwww.hotelsherazade.com. Before riads took off big time, this place was already on the scene, an old merchant's house prettily done up. Besides a lovely roof terrace, the hotel offers a wide variety of well-maintained rooms, not all en suite. Run very professionally by a German-Moroccan couple, it's extremely popular with European visitors, so book well ahead. Prices tend to be on the high side compared with the competition (the *Gallia* and the *Jnane Mogador*), with a range of rooms starting at 260dh, not including breakfast.

Hotel Souria 17 Rue de la Recette ☎075 28 80 17. Deservedly popular family-run hotel. The rooms, set around a pleasant patio, are small and well kept, but the real reason why people like this place is

because the women who run it make you feel like a guest in their own home. Hot showers cost 10dh. Double rooms 130dh; breakfast not included.

Jnane Mogador Hotel Derb Sidi Bouloukat, by 116 Rue Riad Zitoun el Kadim ☎ & ℻044 42 63 23, ⓦwww.jnanemogador.com. Run by the same management as the *Essaouira*, this more upmarket hostelry is just as homely and is already establishing itself as a favourite among Marrakesh's mid-range accommodation. Set in a beautifully restored old house, it boasts charming rooms around a lovely fountain patio, its own hammam and a roof terrace where you can have breakfast, or tea and cake. Great value; doubles 380dh, though the rate doesn't include breakfast.

Les Jardins de la Medina 21 Derb Chtouka, Kasbah ☎044 38 18 51, ℻044 38 53 85, ⓦwww.lesjardinsdelamedina .com. A beautiful old palace transformed into a truly sumptuous hotel. The thirty-six rooms, each with its own character and individual decor, are set around an extensive patio garden with hammocks slung between the trees and a decent-sized pool. What the hotel really plugs, however, is its hammam-cum-beauty salon where you can get manicured, pedicured, scrubbed and massaged till you glow. Double rooms start at 2100dh.

Riad Blanc 25 Derb Si Said, off Rue Riad Zitoun el Jedid ☎ & ℻044 38 27 60, ⓦwww.riadblanc.com. An old Medina house located between Maison Tiskiwin and Dar Si Said, and restored with just enough stucco, carved cedar and *zellij* to be classic without going over the top. The rooms similarly manage to be stylish without looking over-designed. There's a plunge pool in the patio, a Jacuzzi on the roof, and an in-house hammam. Doubles start at €85.

Riad Kaïss 65 Derb Jedid, off Rue Riad Zitoun el Kadim ☎ & ℻044 44 01 41, ⓦwww.riadkaiss.com. A luxury riad in a nineteenth-century house done out in quite an interesting contemporary Moroccan style – the light, modern decor seamlessly incorporates traditional features such as windows with stained glass in vivid primary colours. Rooms mostly surround a large open courtyard with orange trees, a fountain and recesses with divans to lounge on. There's also a large, cool salon, an in-house hammam, and a multi-level roof terrace with pavilions and a pool. Double rooms start at 1530dh.

Riad Zinoun 31 Derb Ben Amrane, off Rue Riad Zitoun el Kadim ☎ & ⓕ044 42 67 93, ⓦwww.riadzinoun.com. A friendly little riad, run by a French-Moroccan couple. Not the most chic of its kind in the Medina, but very pleasant and set around a patio (covered in winter, open in summer) in a nicely refurbished old house. Doubles from €79.

Riad al Moussika 17 Derb Cherkaoui, off Rue Douar Graoua ☎044 38 90 67, ⓕ044 37 76 53, ⓦwww.riyad-al-moussika ma. A gem of a riad, formerly owned by Thami el Glaoui (see p.76), with absolutely gorgeous decor, all designed to exact specifications in traditional Moroccan style by its Italian owner. The resulting combination of Moroccan tradition and Italian flair is harmonious and beautiful – like a traditional Marrakshi mansion, but better. The walls are decked with contemporary paintings by local artists, and the owner's son, a cordon bleu chef, takes care of the catering – in fact, the riad claims to have the finest cuisine in town. Doubles from €250 including breakfast, lunch and afternoon tea.

Villa des Orangers 6 Rue Sidi Mimoun, off Place Youssef Ben Tachfine ☎044 38 46 38, ⓕ044 38 51 23, ⓦwww.villadesorangers.com. Officially classified as a hotel, this place is in fact a riad in the true sense of the term, an old house around a patio garden (two gardens in fact) – with orange trees and a complete overdose of lovely carved stucco. There's a range of rooms and suites – many with their own private terrace – as well as two pools (one on the roof and the other in the garden), and a spacious salon with a real fireplace. Doubles from 2900dh, including breakfast and a light lunch.

Northern Medina

See map on pp.120–121.

Bordj Dar Lamane 11 Derb El Koudia (aka Derb Kabbadj), off Place Ben Salah ☎044 37 85 41, ⓕ044 33 04 87, ⓦwww.stay-in-a-riad.com. Easy to find from Place Ben Salah (the arch leading to it has a sign painted over it), this is a pleasant little Moroccan-owned riad in an interesting part of the Medina, far enough from the Jemaa el Fna to avoid the tourist throng, but near enough to be there in 10min when you want to be. There are seven rooms around a patio that's covered in winter, open in summer. The decor is based on traditional features such as painted woodwork, and there's a lovely flower-filled roof terrace. English is spoken. Doubles €79.

Dar el Assafir 24bis Arset el Hamed ☎044 38 73 77, ⓕ044 38 68 48, ⓦwww.riadelassafir.com. Located in a rather atypical part of the Medina, behind the town hall, this is a late nineteenth century colonial mansion done out in colonial rather than traditional style. It's quite spacious, with two patios and a nice pool, singing birds in a little aviary and *belle*

▲ LA MAISON ARABE

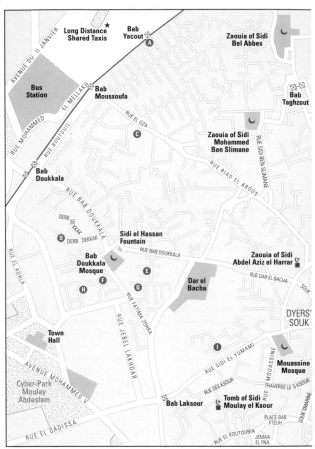

époque-style rooms with orientalist ornaments. Doubles from 1300dh.

Dar Mouassine 148 Derb Essnane, off **Rue Sidi el Yumami** ☏044 44 52 87. The rooms are done out in classic Moroccan decor, the salon and the patio less so, though the latter has a fountain and banana trees. There are well-chosen and interesting prints on the walls, all rooms have CD players, and the better ones have painted wooden ceilings. Doubles start at 850dh.

Dar Salam 162 Derb Ben Fayda, off Rue el Gza near Bab Doukkala ☏ & ℻044 38 31 10, ⓦwww.dar-salam.com. Not really a typical riad, more a Moroccan family home that takes in guests. This is a place

to relax and put your feet up rather than admire the decor, and the food is similarly unpretentious – tasty home-style Moroccan cooking like your mum would make if she were Marrakshi. The price is also a lot more homely than in most riads, with double rooms at €40.

La Maison Arabe 1 Derb Assebbe **Bab Doukkala, behind the Doukkala Mosque** ☏044 38 70 10, ℻044 38 72 21, ⓦwww.lamaisonarabe.com. Though not as famous as the *Mamounia*, this is arguably Marrakesh's classiest hotel, boasting high standards of service in a gorgeous nineteenth-century mansion that's been newly restored with fine traditional

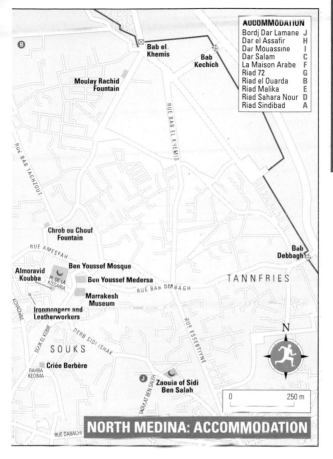

NORTH MEDINA: ACCOMMODATION

ACCOMMODATION	
Bordj Dar Lamane	J
Dar el Assafir	H
Dar Mouassine	I
Dar Salam	C
La Maison Arabe	F
Riad 72	G
Riad el Ouarda	B
Riad Malika	E
Riad Sahara Nour	D
Riad Sindibad	A

workmanship. The furnishings are classic Moroccan and sumptuous, as is the food (this was a restaurant before it was a hotel, and it even offers cookery classes). There are two beautifully kept patios and a selection of rooms and suites, all with TV, minibar, a/c and heating, some with private terrace and Jacuzzi. There is no pool on the premises, but a free shuttle bus can take you to the hotel's private pool nearby. Doubles from 1900dh, including breakfast and afternoon tea.

Riad 72 72 Derb Arset Aouzal ☎044 38 76 29, ☏044 38 47 18, ⊛www.riad72 .com. A very sleek and stylish riad, with sparse but extremely tasteful modern decor,

palms and banana trees in the courtyard and its own hammam (but no pool). The catering is Moroccan. Doubles from €144 including breakfast and afternoon tea.

Riad el Ouarda 5 Derb Taht Sour Lakbir, near the Zaouia of Sidi Bel Abbes ☎044 38 57 14, ☏044 38 57 10, ⊛www.riadelouarda.com. A stylish riad in a seventeenth-century house with lots of original features, including oodles of stucco, painted wooden doors and ceilings, zellij floors and lots of klims (woven carpets). The rooms are warm but uncluttered, and the terrace has great views over Sidi Bel Abbes and the Medina. Double rooms cost 1500dh.

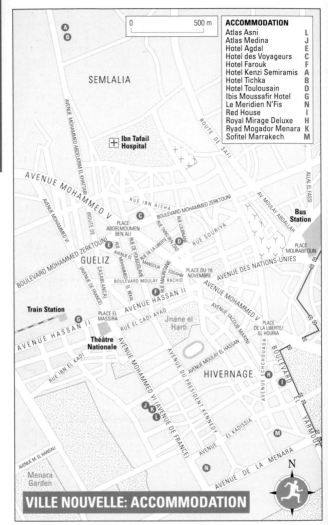

VILLE NOUVELLE: ACCOMMODATION

Riad Malika 29–36 Derb Arset Aouzal ☎ & ⓕ 044 44 38 51, ⓦ www.riadmalika .com. Sumptuous decor – modern but with colonial and 1930s touches – bedecks this very stylish riad owned by architect and interior designer Jean-Luc Lemée. There's loads of checkered tiling, a lovely pool, a warm salon and plush bedroom furnishings. It's very popular and needs booking

well ahead; if it's full, Jean-Luc does run another, almost equally good riad – *Dar Doukkala* – very nearby at 83 Rue Bab Doukkala. Doubles start at €125.

Riad Sahara Nour 118 Derb Dekkak ☎ 044 37 65 70, ⓦ www.riadsaharanour -marrakech.com. More than just a riad, this is a centre for art, self-development and relaxation. Art workshops in music, dance, painting and calligraphy are held here, with the emphasis on a cross-fertilization of European, African and Middle-Eastern ideas; self-development programmes are available including those in meditation and relaxation techniques. Guests who wish to hold artistic happenings are encouraged. However you don't need to take part in these activities in order to stay here; you can enjoy the calm atmosphere on the patio, shaded by orange, loquat and pomegranate trees. Doubles from €75.

Riad Sindibad 413 Arset Ben Brahim, just inside Bab Yacout ☎ & ☏ 044 38 13 10, ⊛ www.riad-sindibad.com. Thoughtfully done up by its French owners, with Moroccan touches, the feel here remains predominantly European. The rooms, set around an intimate patio with a small pool, are comfortable and en suite, and there's a Jacuzzi and hammam on the roof terrace. The location is a bit of a way from the main Medina sights, however. Doubles from €90.

Ville Nouvelle

See map on p.122.

Guéliz

Hotel Agdal 1 Bd Mohammed Zerktouni ☎ 044 43 36 70, ☏ 044 43 12 39. One of the better Guéliz hotels, with a pool, bar and restaurant; well situated for the restaurants and cafés around Place Abdelmoumen Ben Ali. Rooms are smallish but have a/c, satellite TV and balcony. Doubles 580dh, not including breakfast.

Hotel des Voyageurs 40 Bd Mohammed Zerktouni ☎ 044 44 72 18. Has rather an old-fashioned feel, but it's well kept, with spacious rooms and a pleasant little garden. Quiet and peaceful despite being located right in the heart of Guéliz. Doubles from 160dh, not including breakfast.

Hotel Farouk 66 Av Hassan II ☎ 044 43 19 89, ☏ 044 44 05 22, ℮ hotelfarouk @hotmail.com. Owned by the same family as the *Ali* (see p.115), this is the top choice for a budget hotel in the Ville Nouvelle. A slightly eccentric building, with all sorts of branches and extensions, it offers a variety of rooms – have a look at a few before choosing all with hot showers. Staff are

friendly and welcoming, and there's an excellent restaurant. Doubles 150dh.

Hotel Toulousain 44 Rue Tariq Ben Ziad ☎ 044 43 00 33, ☏ 044 43 14 46, ⊛ www.geocities.com/hotel_toulousain. Located behind the municipal market, this budget hotel was originally owned by a Frenchman from Toulouse (hence the name), and has a secure car park and a variety of rooms, some with shower, some with shower and toilet, some with shared facilities. Doubles start at 170dh.

Ibis Moussafir Hotel Av Hassan II/Place de la Gare ☎ 044 43 59 29 to 32, ☏ 044 43 59 36, ⊛ www.ibishotel.com. Part of a chain of modern, largely business-oriented hotels. Not the most exciting accommodation in town, but good value, with efficient service, a swimming pool, a restaurant, a bar in the lobby and good buffet breakfasts included in the rate. Doubles 546dh.

Hivernage

Atlas Asni Av Mohammed VI (Av de France) ☎ 044 33 99 00, ☏ 044 42 00 09, ⊛ www.hotelsatlas.com. A decent four-star, and one of the largest and best known of the Hivernage hotels. Though outwardly bleak and barracks-like, it has cool fresh rooms, a buffet restaurant and a coffee shop offering Italian-style snacks. The hotel also provides a swimming pool and fitness club, plus access to the spa facilities of its nearby sister hotel, the *Atlas Medina*. There are also two bars, and a nightclub, *the Alcazar*, featuring Middle Eastern-style cabaret acts. Most importantly, the hotel is known for its efficient staff and high standards of service. Doubles 1150dh not including breakfast.

Atlas Medina Av Moulay el Hassan ☎ 044 33 99 99, ☏ 044 42 00 99, ⊛ www.hotelsatlas.com. Set amid extensive gardens – five hectares, planted with no less than 200 palm trees – this is the Atlas chain's top offering in Marrakesh. It's best known for its spa facilities which incorporate treatments using traditional Moroccan hammam cosmetics such as *ghassoul* mud-shampoo, here used for a facial rather than to wash hair. The lobby is very stylish, done out in terracotta with Art Deco-style touches and Berber motifs; the rooms are quite plush, with a warmer feel, though still incorporating the same styles. Doubles from 2000dh not including breakfast.

Le Meridien N'Fis Av Mohammed VI (Av de France) ☎044 33 94 00, ℱ044 33 94 05, ✆www.lemeridien.com. The rooms here are nothing special, though they do have satellite TV, a/c and heating. The public areas are quite tastefully decorated, however, and the hotel boasts its own pool, hammam, sauna, fitness centre and creche, plus five restaurants. Two rooms are adapted for wheelchair users. Doubles 3700dh, not including breakfast, but there are often promotional rates.

Royal Mirage Deluxe Rue Echchouada (Rue de Paris) ☎044 42 54 00, ℱ044 42 54 42, ✆www.royalmiragehotels. com. A small, decidedly deluxe hotel, priding itself on its personalized service, with features such as an in-room movie service and high-speed internet access. The public areas are quite palatial, with rich decor and lots of red carpet, painted ceilings and *zellij* tiling, and the rooms aren't bad either, apart from the horrible imitation-wood laminate flooring. In principle, doubles cost 5000dh, but promotional rates are often available.

Ryad Mogador Menara Av Mohammed VI (Av de France) ☎044 33 93 30, ℱ044 33 93 33, ✆www.ryadmogador. com. Spanking new five-star whose facilities include a health club and three restaurants but, in deference to religious sensibilities, sale and consumption of alcohol are banned on the premises. The lobby is done out in classic style, with painted ceilings, chandeliers and a very Moroccan feel, and the receptionists wear traditional garb. Rooms, on the other hand, are modern, light and airy. For those with children in tow, there's a babysitting service. There are four rooms adapted for wheelchair users. Doubles go for 1600dh.

Sofitel Marrakech Rue Harroun Errachid ☎044 42 56 02 or 03, ℱ044 42 05 05, ✆www.sofitel.com. Quite a classy five-star incorporating classical elements into the design of both its exterior and its grand rooms, all done out in royal red. It also has 61 suites, and four rooms adapted for wheelchair users, plus two restaurants, two bars and a fitness centre with a sauna, Jacuzzi and hammam. Double rooms start at 2950dh.

The Red House Bd el Yarmouk opposite the city wall ☎044 43 70 40 or 41, ℱ044 44 74 09, ✆www.theredhouse -marrakech.com. A beautiful nineteenth-century mansion (also called *Dar el Ahmar*) full of fine stucco and *zellij* work downstairs, where the restaurant offers gourmet Moroccan cuisine. Accommodation consists of

▲ RIAD AL MOUSSIKA

eight luxurious suites – extremely chic and palatial – though European imperial rather than classic Moroccan in style. Doubles from 2500dh.

Semlalia

Hotel Kenzi Semiramis Off Av Mohammed Abdelkrim el Khattabi (Route de Casablanca) ☎044 43 13 77, ℱ044 44 71 27, ﹫www.kenzi-hotels.com. Part of the Moroccan Kenzi chain which specializes in sports holidays. Though there are facilities for tennis, badminton, *pétanque* and even archery, the main sport here is golf, and the hotel runs a free shuttle bus (daily except Sun & public hols) to the nearby Amelkis golf course. The hotel has a relaxed and comfortable feel throughout: the lobby is an atrium with a multi-level desert-style garden; the rooms are understatedly luxurious; and the staff are friendly and courteous. Four rooms are adapted for wheelchair users. Doubles cost 1850dh excluding breakfast, with promotional rates often available.

Hotel Tichka Off Mohammed Abdelkrim el Khattabi ☎044 44 87 10, ℱ044 44 86 91, ﹫www.salamhotelsmaroc.com. Built in 1986, this hotel boasts fine architecture and decor by Tunisian architect Charles Boccara and the acclaimed American interior designer Bill Willis, including columns in the form of stylized palm trees that are reminiscent of ancient Egypt, or even Art Deco. Most notable is the use of a super-smooth, beautifully coloured plaster glaze called *tadelakt*, which was traditionally used in hammams to waterproof the walls, and whose use here by Willis made it massively trendy in Moroccan interior design. All rooms have a/c, heating, satellite TV and a mini-bar; the hotel has a swimming pool, a health centre and its own hammam. The staff are friendly but the hotel is getting a bit worn around the edges. Doubles 1400dh, excluding breakfast.

The Palmery

Dar Zemora 72 Rue el Aandalib ☎044 32 82 00, ℱ044 32 82 01, ﹫www .darzemora.com. A British-owned luxury villa stylishly done out with a mix of traditional and modern features. There's a pleasant garden with a heated pool, a masseur on call and a view of the Atlas mountains from the roof terrace. All rooms have CD players though no TV. To find it, take the next left (Rue Qortoba) off the Route de Fes after the Circuit de la Palmeraie, then the first right (Rue el Yassamin), fork left after 300m and it's 300m round the bend on the right. Doubles 2420dh including breakfast and afternoon tea.

Hotel Palmeraie Golf Palace Circuit de la Palmeraie, off Route de Casablanca ☎044 30 10 10, ℱ044 30 50 50, ﹫www.pgpmarrakech.com. One of the better five-stars, though some way out of town, the *Palmeraie Golf Palace* has no fewer than five swimming pools, plus squash and tennis courts, a bowling alley, riding stables, and most importantly, its own eighteen-hole golf course. A favourite with Morocco's late king, Hassan II, the hotel is known for its high standard of service. The rooms are elegant and split-level, with beds raised above the sitting area. Doubles from 4680dh, not including breakfast.

Les Deux Tours Douar Abiad, Circuit de la Palmeraie ☎044 32 95 25 to 27, ℱ044 32 95 23, ﹫www.lesdeuxtours .net. The *deux tours* (two towers) of the name flank the gateway to this cluster of luxury *villas d'hôte* designed by locally renowned architect Charles Boccara. Though located in rather a raggedy patch of the palmery, and not signposted (take a turn-off to the east about halfway along the Route de la Palmeraie, signposted "Villa des Trois Golfs", then continue for about 400m, ignoring any further signs to the *Trois Golfs*), this is a beautiful, tranquil spot, with four rooms to each villa, all built in traditional Moroccan brick and done out in restful earth colours, each villa with its own little garden. There's a hammam, swimming pool, restaurant and bar as well as extensive shared gardens to wander or relax in. Doubles go for 2000dh half-board.

The Atlas Mountains

Imlil

CAF Refuge By the taxi stand ☎(c/o *Café Aksoual*, opposite) 044 48 56 12.

Clean but spartan, this place is for proper mountaineers, not wimps or softies. Dorm beds at 52dh (or 29dh if you're a Club Alpin Français or Hostelling International member); breakfast isn't included, but there's a kitchen if you want to rustle up your own.

Hotel-Café Soleil ☎044 48 56 22, Ⓔcafesoleil44@yahoo.fr. A cheery little place with bright rooms, friendly staff and great views from the terrace. There are hot showers, but only one room is en suite. Doubles from 150dh.

Kasbah du Toubkal ☎044 48 56 11, Ⓕ044 48 56 36, Ⓦwww.kasbahdutoub-kal.com; UK bookings ☎01883/774392. The former kasbah of a local *caïd* (chief) lovingly restored by British tour company Discover Ltd using local crafts and workers, this is Imlil's top offering and indeed its top sight. It also starred as the Dalai Lama's palace in Martin Scorsese's film *Kundun*, but you don't need to be the leader of Tibet to enjoy the beautiful guest rooms or the excellent meals, nor to take advantage of the excursions it offers, on foot or by mule. Even if you don't stay here, it's worth at least popping in for tea on the terrace. Doubles €140 including use of the in-house hammam.

Setti Fatma

Hotel-Restaurant Asgaour 100m below the taxi stand ☎044 48 52 94. A bright little hotel with rooms above its restaurant, proudly displaying its French guidebook recommendations. The rooms are small and plain but clean and carpeted, some en suite (otherwise, shared hot showers are 5dh), and there's a sunny upper-floor terrace. Doubles from 70dh not including breakfast.

Hotel-Restaurant Sitti Fadma 200m below the taxi stand ☎044 48 54 21. A simple but friendly little place with a big roof terrace and a pleasant garden overlooking the river. Rooms are plain but clean and comfortable, with shared bathroom facilities (hot showers 10dh); there's a restaurant serving food indoors or in the garden. Doubles 70dh excluding breakfast.

La Perle d'Ourika Asgaour, 300m below the taxi stand ☎044 48 52 95. This is as far upmarket as Setti Fatma gets in the way of accommodation, though it's still pretty rustic. The rooms are reasonably clean

and pleasant and most have great views, as does the multi-level terrace restaurant. Doubles from 200dh.

Oukaïmaden

CAF Refuge ☎044 31 90 36. Priority is given to Club Alpin Français members at this hostel, which has the only budget accommodation in the village. You stay in a dorm and there are sheets and blankets, but you're advised to bring a sleeping bag nonetheless. Meals are also available. 95dh per person (60dh for CAF members and for youth hostellers with an HI card).

Hotel de l'Angour (Chez Juju) ☎044 31 90 05, Ⓕ044 48 52 94. There's an old fashioned, almost country-pub feel about this place on the main road in the centre of the village. It's nice and homely with a decent bar and restaurant, some rooms fully en suite, but most with just a shower en suite and a toilet on the landing. Doubles from 680dh full board (which is compulsory at weekends), 580dh half-board.

Kenzi Louka ☎044 31 90 80 to 87, Ⓕ044 31 90 88, Ⓦwww.kenzi-hotels .com. This four-star hotel above the main road into the village is a bit scuffed around the edges, and is used mainly by tour groups, but it's the place to come if you want an indoor swimming pool, an in-house hammam and rooms with TV, mini-bar and conservatory-style glassed-in window-covered balconies. Doubles 900dh excluding breakfast.

Hotel Résidence le Courchevel ☎044 31 90 92. This place is actually made of concrete, but it does give an excellent impression of being built out of wood. There's a largely wooden facade, wood panelling and carpet in all the rooms and it's pretty warm and cosy. There's also a posh restaurant. Doubles 1120dh half-board.

Essaouira

Dar Adul 63 Rue Touahen ☎ & Ⓕ044 47 39 10, Ⓦwww.dar-adul.com. Lashings of whitewash (with maritime blue woodwork) give this riad a bright, airy feel, and help to keep it cool in summer. It's French-run, with a selection of different-sized rooms

– some split-level – and the biggest has a fireplace to keep it warm in winter. Doubles from €55.

Dar al Bahar 1 Rue Touahen ☏ & ☏ 044 47 68 31, ⊛ www.daralbahar.com. Wild views of the ocean crashing against the rocks below, especially from the terrace, plus cool whitewashed rooms, hung with paintings by some of the best local artists, make this riad an excellent choice, though it's a bit tucked away. Doubles from €45.

Hotel Beau Rivage 14 Place Prince Moulay el Hassan ☏ & ☏ 044 47 59 25, ⓔ beaurivage@menara.ma. A former backpackers' hotel which has been completely refurbished and taken a couple of steps upmarket. It has an enviable position right on the main square – which also means that rooms at the front can be a bit noisy at times. There's a variety of charming en-suite rooms, but the price has been hiked more times than the hotel's been refurbished, so it's not great value. Doubles are 400dh without breakfast.

Hotel Riad al Medina 9 Rue Attarine ☏ 044 47 59 07, ☏ 044 47 66 95, ⊛ www.riadalmadina.com. A former palatial mansion built in 1871, this hotel had fallen on hard times by the 1960s and become a budget hotel for hippies. Guests supposedly included Jimi Hendrix (in room 13 according to some stories, room 28 say others), as well as Frank Zappa, the Jefferson Airplane and Cat Stevens. Now refurbished, it has bags of character and helpful staff but it's still rather rustic in some respects (the plumbing can be temperamental for example). Doubles from 814dh excluding breakfast.

Hotel Souiri 37 Rue Attarine ☏ 044 78 30 94, ☏ 044 47 53 39, ⓔ souiri@ menara.ma. Very central and very popular, with a range of rooms, the cheaper ones having shared bathroom facilities. Rooms at the front cost more than those at the back, though the latter are quieter. Doubles start at 250dh.

Hotel Tafraout 7 Rue de Marrakesh ☏ 044 47 62 76. A spotless little budget hotel with friendly staff and comfortable rooms, some en suite, though not all have outside windows. There's hot water in the evenings only, but right next door there are good public hot showers for both sexes. Doubles start at 150dh without breakfast.

Riad le Grand Large 2 Rue Oum Rabia ☏ 044 47 68 86, ☏ 044 47 28 86, ⊛ www.riadlegrandlarge.com. Despite its name, this is a small, cosy place with ten smallish rooms, lovely staff, a classy restaurant and a roof terrace café. Good value, with reductions off season. Doubles 590dh.

Sofitel Thalassa Mogador Bd Mohammed V ☏ 044 47 90 00, ☏ 044 47 90 80, ⊛ www.sofitel.com. The most expensive hotel in Essaouira by a very long chalk, featuring a pool, two bars, two restaurants and a thalassotherapy centre (in case a good old-fashioned swim in the sea isn't thalassotherapeutic enough). One room is adapted for wheelchair users. Double rooms are 2480dh, not including breakfast.

Villa Maroc 10 Rue Abdallah Ben Yassin, just inside the Medina wall near the clocktower ☏ 044 47 61 47, ☏ 044 47 58 06, ⊛ www.villa-maroc.com. An upmarket riad comprising two old houses converted into a score of rooms and suites. Established long before riads became trendy, it's decorated with the finest Moroccan materials and even has its own hammam. The villa is accessible only on foot, though there are porters on hand to carry your luggage from the car park in Place Orson Welles. Most of the year you will need to book several months ahead to stay here. Double rooms 850dh including breakfast.

Essentials

Arrival and transport

Marrakesh's **Menara airport** is 4km southwest of town. The arrivals hall should have bank kiosks to change money and ATMs to extract cash using plastic; during recent renovations these have been closed, so you may not be able to obtain Moroccan money immediately upon arrival. However this shouldn't be too much of a problem as taxis will accept euros (and sometimes dollars or sterling) at more or less the equivalent dirham rate; alternatively you can always have them call by an ATM en route to your destination.

Petits taxis, which you can pick up in front of the airport terminal, may try to overcharge you. It shouldn't cost more than 50dh to reach the Jemaa el Fna or central Guéliz, and it would cost less if you could get the driver to agree to use the meter (he almost certainly won't). Shared *grands taxis*, which also wait in front of the airport building, charge around 60dh for up to six passengers for the trip to the Jemaa el Fna, Guéliz and Hivernage (the price is posted up on a board, which you can point to if need be). The #11 bus is supposed to run half-hourly until around 10pm from the stop in front of the airport terminal to the Jemaa el Fna (3dh), but the service is not always reliable.

Transport

The easiest way to get around town is to ride in one of the beige **petits taxis**. These take up to three passengers and are equipped with a meter; if the driver doesn't use it, it's because he intends to overcharge you. Most trips around town (*petits taxis* are not allowed beyond the city limits) cost 5–15dh, or 8–20dh at night, when there is a fifty-percent surcharge on the metered fare. If you're a lone passenger, it's standard practice for the driver to pick up one or two additional passengers en route, each of whom will pay the full fare for their journey, as will you. There are *petit taxi* ranks at most major intersections in Guéliz, and in the Medina in the northwest corner of the Jemaa el Fna, at the junction of Avenue Houman el Fetouaki and Rue Oqba Ben Nafia, and at the Place des Ferblantiers end of Avenue Houman el Fetouaki.

Grands taxis

Grands taxis – typically large Mercedes' – usually run as shared taxis, taking six passengers (though only designed for four) for a fixed price. You'll probably only want to use a *grand taxi* if you're heading to the Atlas mountains or to Essaouira.

Bike rental

An alternative for exploring the more scattered sights, such as the Agdal and Menara gardens or the palmery, is a **bicycle**, **moped** or **scooter**. You can rent bicycles from Bazar Salah Eddine next to *Hotel Souria* in the Medina, and from a number of roadside locations in Hivernage, most notably at the junction of Avenue el Kaissia (also spelt Qadassia) with Avenue du Président Kennedy, and also on the east side of Place de la Liberté. Mopeds and scooters can be rented at Marrakesh Motos (aka Chez Jamal Boucetta), 100m up the street at 34 Av Mohammed Abdelkrim el Khattabi (T044 44 83 59). Loc2Roues on the upper floor of Galerie Élite, 212 Av Mohammed V (T044 43 02 94, W www.loc2roues .com) rents out mopeds and scooters. Expect to pay around 100dh a day for a bicycle, 300dh for a moped or scooter.

Getting around town by bike is easy, but be aware that Moroccan drivers are not the world's best. In particular, do not expect them to observe lane discipline, nor to indicate when turning or changing lanes.

Fly Less – Stay Longer!

Rough Guides believes in the good that travel does, but we are deeply aware of the impact of fuel emissions on climate change. We recommend taking fewer trips and staying for longer. If you can avoid travelling by air, please use an alternative, especially for journeys of under 1000km/600miles. And always offset your travel at roughguides.com/climatechange.

Grands taxis operate from various ranks around the city, each of which is designated for certain routes. When you arrive at the departure point, ask which vehicle is going to your destination and, unless you want to charter the whole taxi, make clear that you just want individual seats (*une place* for one person, *deux places* for two and so on).

It's possible to **charter** a *grand taxi* by paying for all six places. Negotiate the price in advance; if your destination isn't one covered by a regular taxi run, the cost should be roughly equivalent to six fares on a standard journey of that distance.

Grands taxis are fast for journeys out of town, but they are cramped and drivers are prone to speeding and overtaking on blind curves or the brows of hills. They have more than their fair share of crashes in a country where the road accident rate is already high. A lot of accidents involve *grand taxi* drivers falling asleep at the wheel at night,

so you may wish to avoid travelling by *grand taxi* after dark.

Calèches

Calèches – horse-drawn cabs – line up near the Koutoubia, the El Badi Palace and some of the fancier hotels. They take up to five people and are not much more expensive than *petits taxis* – though be sure to fix the price in advance, particularly if you want a tour of the town. Expect to pay around 200dh an hour, or 300dh for a tour round the Medina walls, less if you bargain hard.

Buses

City buses are cheap and efficient. The routes you are most likely to want to use are #1 and #16, which run along Avenue Mohammed V between Guéliz and the Koutoubia. Other handy routes include #6 and #20 from Avenue Mohammed V via Bab Ighli to the Agdal gardens, and #11 from the Koutoubia to the Menara gardens and the airport.

Sightseeing bus tour

If you don't have much time and you want to scoot around Marrakesh's major sights in a day or two, the **hop-on hop-off Marrakech Tour bus** could be for you. Using open-top double-deckers, with a commentary in several languages including English, the tour follows two circular routes: the first tours the Medina and Guéliz, calling at Place Foucauld (for the Jemaa and Koutoubia), Place des Ferblantiers (for the Bahia and El Badi Palaces, plus the Mellah), and the Menara gardens; the second tours the palmery, following the Circuit de la Palmeraie. The medina/Guéliz bus departs from outside Boule de Neige café in Place Abdelmoumen Ben Ali every 30min from 9am till 5pm; the palmery bus leaves from the same place every 80min from 9.50am till 3.50pm. You can get on and off where you like, and tickets (costing 130dh) can be bought on board, or at Place Abdelmoumen Ben Ali or Place Foucauld. They are valid for 24hr, so even if you start your tour after lunch, you can finish it the following morning. For further details, call ☎ 044 33 52 70 or 72, or log onto ⓦ www.marrakech-tour.com (though the website is currently available only in French or Spanish).

Information

The **Moroccan National Tourist Office** (Office National Marocain de Tourisme in French or ONMT for short; @ www .tourisme-marocain.com) has offices in several Western cities including London (☎ 020/7437 0073, @ www.visitmorocco .org), Orlando, Florida (☎ 407/264 0133), Montreal (☎ 514/842 8111) and Sydney (☎ 02/9922 4999). As well as providing specific information, these offices stock a number of pamphlets on the main Moroccan cities and resorts, and a few items on cultural themes.

The ONMI office in Marrakesh, also called the **Délégation Régional du Tourisme**, is on Place Abdelmoumen Ben Ali in Guéliz (Mon–Fri 9am–4.30pm, Sat 9am–noon & 3–6pm; ☎ 044 43 62 39). The staff are generally helpful, and keep a dossier of useful information with listings of hotels, campsites, car-rental firms and other useful contacts.

A number of Marrakesh city **maps** are available, including Rough Guides' own Marrakesh map, which is printed on tear-proof paper, and is the best map of the city that you'll get. It's most easily available abroad, but a few places in Marrakesh sell it, including Librairie Chatr (see p.91) and Hanan Internet (see p.136). Among locally produced maps, the best is Marocity's "Plan Guide Map", costing around 15dh.

Marrakesh websites

The best website for Marrakesh information is the I Love Marrakech site at @ www.ilovemarrakech.com, with pages on the city's history, golf in Marrakesh, the latest weather forecast and Marrakesh news. Add a hyphen to the URL and change the spelling of the city's name, and you reach the much more commercial oriented @ www .ilove-marrakech.com, where you'll find listings for upmarket hotels, riads and restaurants, plus write-ups and some photos of the main tourist sights. Finally, @ www.elhamra.com has some useful listings of clinics, dental practices, travel agencies and car rental firms, among others.

Hiring a guide

A local guide can help you find things in the Medina, and a good guide can give some interesting commentary, but you certainly don't need one. Armed with this book, and a good map, you can easily find your way around Marrakesh and check out all the sights on your own. Should you want one however, **official guides** (150dh for half a day) can be engaged at the ONMT or large hotels. Although it's illegal to work as an unofficial guide, unlicensed guides can be found in the Jemaa el Fna, and will suddenly appear almost anywhere in the Medina if you're seen looking perplexed.

When hiring a guide, be precise about exactly what you want to see and, with an unlicensed guide, agree a fee very clearly at the outset. Whether official or not, most guides will want to steer you into shops which pay them **commission** on anything you buy (added to your bill, of course). Be wary as this commission is not small – official guides quite commonly demand as much as fifty percent. You should therefore make it very clear from the start if you do not want to visit any shops or carpet "museums". Don't be surprised if your guide subsequently loses interest or tries to raise the fee.

Money

Morocco's unit of currency is the **dirham** (dh), which at the time of writing was selling at approximately 16dh for £1, 9dh for US$1, 11dh for €1. As with all currencies there are fluctuations, but the dirham has roughly held its own against Western currencies over the last few years. The dirham is divided into 100 **centimes** or francs, and you may find prices written or expressed in centimes rather than dirhams. Confusingly, prices are sometimes quoted in **rials**, one rial being five centimes. Coins of 5, 10, 20 and 50 centimes, and 1, 5 and 10 dirhams are in circulation, along with notes of 20, 50, 100 and 200 dirhams. It is illegal to import or export Moroccan dirhams, and they are not easily obtainable abroad.

US and Canadian dollars and pounds sterling (Bank of England – not Scottish or Northern Irish notes) are easily exchangeable at Marrakesh banks, but **euros** are by far the best hard currency to carry, since they are not only easy to change, but are accepted as cash very widely, at the rate of €1 for 10dh. **Traveller's cheques** are more secure because you can get them replaced if stolen.

The main area for **banks** in the Medina is off the south side of the Jemaa el Fna on Rue Moulay Ismail (BMCE and WAFA) and Rue Bab Agnaou (Banque Populaire, SGMB and Credit du Maroc). In Guéliz, the main area is along Av Mohammed V between Place Abdelmoumen Ben Ali and the market. Most major branches have ATMs that will accept foreign cards. **Banking hours** are typically Mon–Thurs 8.15–11.30am & 2.15–5pm and Fri 8.15–11.15am & 2.45– 5pm. However, note that BMCE's branches in Guéliz (144 Av Mohammed V), the Medina (Rue Moulay Ismail on Pl Foucault) and Hivernage (Av de France, opposite *Hotel Atlas*) also have bureaux de change which open daily 8.30am–12.30pm & 3–7pm. The post office will change cash during opening hours (in the Jemaa el Fna, the bureau de change is round the back, by the telephones), and WAFA bank in Rue Moulay Ismail on Place Foucault has a bureau de change open Mon–Fri 8am– 7pm, Sat 9am–1pm & 2–6pm, Sun 9am–4pm. Even outside these hours, the *Hotel Ali* (see p.115) and most upmarket hotels will change traveller's cheques and major hard currencies, though the posh hotels are likely to give bad rates.

Credit and debit cards

Credit and debit cards belonging to the Visa, Mastercard, Cirrus and Plus networks can be used to withdraw cash from **ATMs** across town. If you intend to use your plastic, make sure before you leave home that your cards and personal identification numbers (PINs) will work overseas. You can also settle bills in upmarket hotels, restaurants and tourist shops using Mastercard, Visa or American Express cards.

There is usually a weekly limit on cash withdrawals using your card, typically around 5000dh per week, so you may want to carry some cash as a backup or in case your card is lost or stolen (in which event, cancel it immediately). Note that ATM withdrawals or cash advances obtained with a credit card are treated as loans, with interest accruing daily from the date of withdrawal. By using plastic in ATMs, you get somewhat better exchange rates than those charged by banks for converting cash. Your card issuer may add a foreign transaction fee of as much as 5.5 percent, worth checking before you travel, but you should still get a better deal using an ATM than changing cash in a bank.

Post, phones and email

The main **post office** (*la poste* in French, *el boosta* in Arabic) is on Pl 16 Novembre, midway down Av Mohammed V in Guéliz (Mon–Fri 8.30am–6.30pm, Sat 8.30am–noon). Here you can buy stamps, send letters and collect poste restante (general delivery) mail. There is a separate office, round the side, for sending parcels. The Medina has a branch post office on the Jemaa el Fna (Mon–Thurs 8.30am–noon & 2.30–6.30pm, Fri 8.30–11.30am & 3–6.30pm, Sat 8.30–11.30am).

The easiest way to make a phone call is to buy a **phonecard** (*télécarte*), available from most tobacconists and many newsstands in denominations of 20dh, 30dh, 60dh and 99dh. The cards can be used for local or international calls from public phones all over town (there's a whole army of them by the Jemaa el Fna post office). Another way to make a call is to use a **téléboutique** (they're dotted around town – a couple can be found on Rue Bab Agnaou off the Jemaa el Fna), where you make a call and pay for it when you finish. Calling direct from your hotel room is obviously more convenient, but will cost a lot more.

You may well be able to use your **mobile phone** in Marrakesh, though US phones need to be GSM to work abroad; check with your phone provider if their roaming agreements cover Morocco. Note that once in Marrakesh you'll pay to receive calls as well as to make them. Prepaid cards from abroad cannot be charged up or replaced locally, but you can buy a local SIM card (30dh), which could be handy if you need to make plenty of overseas calls or if you expect to receive calls from the Moroccan network. You can buy SIM cards from offices of Maroc Telecom and Méditel, but you'll need your passport to do so.

To **call abroad from Morocco**, dial ☎0044 for the UK, ☎00353 for Ireland, ☎0061 for Australia or ☎0064 for New Zealand, followed by the area code (minus the initial zero) and the number. To call North America, dial ☎001, then the three-digit area code, then the number. When calling Marrakesh from abroad, dial the international access code, then country code for Morocco, ☎212, followed by the number – omitting the initial zero.

If you're **calling within Morocco**, note that Moroccan area codes have been scrapped, and that all Moroccan phones, including mobiles, now have a nine-digit number, all digits of which must be dialled. Marrakesh landline numbers begin 044, in place of the old 04 area code.

Getting online

There are a growing number of **cybercafés** around town, especially around the Jemaa el Fna; expect to pay around 7–10dh for an hour online. Note that Internet connections can be slow as cybercafés often have too many terminals for the bandwidth available, so it's best to turn up during a quiet period, such as first thing in the morning.

One of the best places to get online is at the Moulay Abdeslam Cyber-Park, on Av Mohammed V opposite the Ensemble Artisanal (Mon–Sat 9.30am–8pm, Sun 10am–6pm). There's a super-modern internet office, with fast connections and low rates (5dh/hr) though, annoyingly, you have to guess how much time you're going to use and pay for it in advance. There are also public phones with computer screens around the park that will connect you to the internet if you have a phonecard; almost the entire park, especially the area near the internet office, is a free wi-fi zone.

Otherwise, cybercafés around the Jemaa el Fna include Cyber Mohamed

Yassine, 36 Rue Bab Agnaou (daily 6am–1am), and Hanan Internet at the southern end of Rue Bab Agnaou (daily 9am–1am). Faster and slightly cheaper is Cyber Club underneath the café opposite the Koutoubia on Av Mohammed V by *Pizza Venezia* (daily 9am–midnight).

In Guéliz, cybercafés are surprisingly thin on the ground; try Jawal, in a yard behind the CTM office on Boulevard Mohammed Zerktouni (daliy 8.30am–midnight), the Café Siraoua a couple of doors down (daily 9am–9pm), or Espace Internet, in the basement at 185 Av Mohammed V (daily 9am–midnight)

Opening hours, holidays and festivals

Shops in the Medina tend to open every day from 9am to 6pm, with some closed for lunch (around 1–3pm), especially on a Friday. In the Ville Nouvelle, shops are much more likely to close for lunch, but tend to stay open later, until 7 or 8pm, and to close on Sundays. Offices are usually open Monday to Thursday 8.30am to noon and 2.30 to 6.30pm; on Friday their hours are typically 8.30 to 11.30am and 3 to 6.30pm. Restaurants generally open between noon and 3pm, and again from 7 to 11pm; only the cheaper places stay open through the afternoon.

All these opening hours change completely during the holy month of **Ramadan** (which starts around 13 Sept 2007, 1 Sept 2008, 22 Aug 2009, 11 Aug 2010), when Muslims fast from daybreak to nightfall. At this time, shops, offices and banks stay open through the

Public holidays in Morocco

Islamic religious holidays occur according to the Muslim lunar calendar, in which months begin when the new moon is sighted. Dates for these holidays in the Western (Gregorian) calendar are impossible to predict exactly, so they may vary by a day or two from the approximate dates given here. The main ones (each involving two days' public holiday) are:

Aid el Kebir	Around 19 Dec 2007, 7 Dec 2008, 26 Nov 2009, 15 Nov 2010.
Aid es Seghir	Around 12 Oct 2007, 30 Nov 2008, 20 Sept 2009, 9 Sept 2010.

Other public holidays are:

New Year's Day	Jan 1
Anniversary of Independence Manifesto	Jan 11
Labour Day	May 1
Feast of the Throne	July 30
King and People's Revolution Day	Aug 20
Allegiance Day	Aug 14
King's Birthday and Youth Day	Aug 21
Anniversary of the Green March	Nov 6
Independence Day	Nov 18

middle of the day and close at 3 or 4pm to allow staff to go home to break the fast. Restaurants may close completely during Ramadan, or open after dusk only, though a couple of places on the Jemaa el Fna will be open through the day to serve tourists.

The biggest religious festivals are **Aïd el Kebir**, celebrating the prophet Abraham's willingness to sacrifice his son to God; and **Aïd es Seghir**, celebrating the end of Ramadan. For both these festivals, shops and offices will be closed for two days. The main secular holiday is the **Feast of the Throne**, celebrating the king's accession.

Marrakesh has three important annual events of its own. The **Marrakesh Marathon** (@ www.marathon-marrakech .com) takes place on the third or fourth Sunday in January, the circuit taking 5000 competitors through the palmery and around the Medina. In June or July, the El Badi Palace and other venues in the city host a two-week **Festival National des Arts Populaires** (@ www.ucam.ac.ma /fnap-aga) featuring performances by musicians and dancers from all over Morocco and beyond, plus spectacular displays of horsemanship each evening at Bab Jedid west of the Koutoubia. November sees the **Marrakesh Film Festival** (@ www .festivalmarrakech.com), in which the featured movies are shown at cinemas across town, and on large screens in the El Badi Palace and the Jemaa el Fna.

Cultural hints

Don't assume that everyone who approaches you on the street in Marrakesh is a **hustler**. Too many visitors do, and end up making little contact with some of the most hospitable people in the world. In any case, in recent years the hustlers have largely been cleared off the streets by police action. Those that remain include a few dope dealers and confidence tricksters, but most will simply be aiming to have you engage them as unofficial guides (see box, p.133).

It's often said that women are second-class citizens in Morocco and other Islamic countries, but Muslim women are usually keen to point out that this is a misinterpretation of women's position in Muslim society. In some ways the sexes are not as unequal as they seem: men traditionally rule in the street, which is their domain, the women's being the home.

Some **women travellers** experience constant sexual harassment, while others have little or no trouble. The obvious strategies for getting rid of unwanted attention are the same as you would use at home: appear confident and assured and you'll avoid a lot of trouble. Moroccan women are traditionally coy and aloof. You should also avoid physical contact with Moroccan men, even in a manner that would not be considered sexual at home, since it could easily be misunderstood. On the other hand, if a Moroccan man touches you he has definitely crossed the line, and you should not be afraid to **make a scene**. Shouting *chooma!* ("shame on you!") is likely to result in bystanders intervening on your behalf.

Visitors of both sexes should be aware of the importance of **appropriate dress**. It is true that in cities some Moroccan women wear short-sleeved tops and knee-length skirts (and may suffer more harassment as a result), and men do wear sleeveless T-shirts and above-the-knee shorts. However, the strict Muslim idea of modest dress requires women to be covered from wrist to ankle, and men from above the elbow to below the knee. The best guide is to note how most Moroccans dress, not how other tourists choose to. For women, wearing long sleeves, long skirts and baggy rather than tight clothes will give an impression of respectability.

Wearing a headscarf to cover your hair and ears gives this impression even more. You may, on the other hand, want to balance this against the heat factor, or you may of course feel that you do not need to make yourself look respectable for the benefit of religious conservatives.

Photography needs to be undertaken with care. If you are obviously taking a photograph of someone, ask their permission. In places much frequented by tourists, you'll often find that local people will demand money for the privilege, especially in the Jemaa el Fna, where bystanders who spot you taking a photograph in which they might feature may be aggressive in asking for money. On a positive note, taking a photograph of someone you've struck up a friendship with and sending it on to them, or exchanging photographs, is often greatly appreciated.

If you're invited to a home, you normally take your **shoes** off before entering the reception rooms – follow your host's lead. It is customary to take a gift: sweet pastries or tea and sugar are always acceptable. If you're **dining**, handle food with your **right hand**; the left is used for "unclean" functions such as wiping your bottom or washing your feet.

During **Ramadan**, when most people are committed to fasting, it's a good idea to be discreet about eating, drinking and smoking during the daytime, and best if possible to confine those activities to your hotel room. Finally, note that in Morocco non-Muslims are excluded from **mosques**, which are regarded as set aside specifically for prayer. Non-Muslims are also excluded from *zaouias*, saints' tombs and some cemeteries.

Directory

Airlines Atlas Blue, Menara airport ☎044 42 42 22; British Airways, Menara airport ☎044 44 89 51; Royal Air Maroc, 197 Av Mohammed V ☎044 42 55 00 or 01; Regional Air Lines, Menara airport ☎044 43 57 36.

Airport information ☎044 44 78 65.

American Express c/o Voyages Schwartz, Immeuble Moutaouakil, 1 Rue Mauritanie, Guéliz ☎044 43 74 69, ℗044 43 33 21, ℮schwartz@wanadoo.net.ma (Mon–Fri 9am–12.30pm & 3–6.30pm, Sat 9am–12.30pm); also c/o S'Tours, Immeuble F, 61 Rue de Yougoslavie, Guéliz ☎044 43 67 46, ℗044 43 67 57, ℮dmc@stours.co .ma (Mon–Fri 8.30am–noon & 2.30–6.30pm, Sat 8.30am–noon).

Bus stations Long-distance buses run by the state-owned CTM (Compagnie des Transports du Maroc; ℺www.ctm.co.ma) operate from their office on Bd Mohammed Zerktouni in Guéliz. Most privately run buses use the *gare routière*, Marrakesh's main bus station, which is just outside the walls of the Medina by Bab Doukkala. It's served by buses #3, #8, #10, #14 or #16 from the Koutoubia. Buses to Essaouira,

Agadir and the Western Sahara run by Supratours, in conjunction with the train company ONCF, run from in front of the train station (see p.140). Note that on long-distance bus journeys you're expected to tip the porters who load your baggage onto buses (5dh – except on CTM, which has charges by weight).

Cookery courses The *Maison Arabe* (see p.120) offers workshops in Moroccan cooking for groups of up to eight people, at 1600dh a day for one or two people and 500–600dh per person for groups of three to eight. It's also possible to learn Moroccan cooking with the Rhode School of Cuisine (UK ☎01252/790 222, US ☎1-888/254 1070, ℺www.rhodeschool ofcuisine.com), who offer week-long courses from \$2395 per person, including villa accommodation in the palmery and meals on site.

Cinemas In Guéliz, the Colisée, alongside the *Café Le Siroua* on Bd Mohammed Zerktouni, is one of the best in town. In the Medina, the Cinéma Mabrouka on Rue Bab Agnaou and the Cinéma Eden, off Rue Riad Zitoun el Jedid, are more downmarket, but watching a film at the Eden in particular is a real Morocco experience. All show a mixture of Hollywood, Bollywood, and some Arabic and French movies, though the Eden still sometimes put on the traditional Bollywood/kung fu double bill – known locally as "*l'histoire et la géographie*".

Clinics Dr Abdelmajid Ben Tbib, 171 Av Mohammed V (☎044 43 10 30) is recommended and speaks English. Dr Frédéric Reitzer, Immeuble Moulay Youssef, Rue de la Liberté, Guéliz (☎044 43 95 62) also speaks some English. Private clinics that have high standards and are accustomed to settling bills with insurance companies include Polyclinque du Sud, at the corner of Rue Yougoslavie and Rue Ibn Aïcha, Guéliz (☎044 44 79 99), and Clinique Yassine, 12 Rue Ibn Toumort (☎044 43 33 23). There's an emergency call-out service, SOS Médecins (☎044 40 40 40), which charges 400dh per consultation.

Consulates France, 1 Rue Ibn Khaldoun ☎044 38 82 00; UK, Honorary Consul at Résidence Taïb, 55 Bd Zerktouni ☎044 43 50 95 (in emergencies only); Sweden, 230 Lotissement Al Masmodi, Targa ☎044 34 33 91.

Customs allowances One litre of wine or spirits and 200 cigarettes.

Dentist Dr Bennani, on the first floor of 112 Av Mohammed V (☎044 44 91 36), opposite the ONMT office in Guéliz, is recommended and speaks some English.

Electricity Most buildings are on 220V but you may still find a 110V supply in some places, and sometimes even both in the same building. Plug sockets are the same as those in France (two round pins), so plugs with square or flat pins will need an adapter, best brought from home, as you won't find one easily in Marrakesh.

Emergencies Fire ☎15; police ☎19. The tourist police (*brigade touristique*; ☎044 38 46 01), set up especially to help tourists, are based at the northern end of Rue Sidi Mimoun, just south of the Koutoubia.

Gay Marrakesh Although sexual segregation makes it relatively widespread, gay sex between men is illegal in Morocco, and attitudes to it are different from those in the West. A Moroccan who takes the dominant role in gay intercourse may well not consider himself to be indulging in a homosexual act, and few Moroccan men will declare themselves gay – which has connotations of femininity and weakness. The idea of being a passive partner on the other hand, is virtually taboo. As for meeting places in Marrakesh, a certain

amount of cruising goes on in the crowds of the Jemaa el Fna in the evening, and there's a gay presence at the *Diamant Noir* nightclub (see p.97). The *Café de la Renaissance* on Pl Abdelmoumen Ben Ali in Guéliz used to be another venue for gay men to meet, but this was closed for renovation at the time of writing. There is no public perception of lesbianism, and opportunities for Western women to make contact with Moroccan lesbians are pretty much nil.

Golf There are three eighteen-hole golf courses in Marrakesh: the Marrakesh Royal Golf Club (☎044 40 98 28, ✉royal_golf @iam.net.ma), 10km out of town on the old Ouarzazate road, which is Morocco's oldest course, opened in 1923 and once played on by the likes of Churchill, Lloyd George and Eisenhower; the Palmeraie Golf Club (☎044 36 87 66, ✉golf@pgp.ma), built, as the name suggests, in the palmery, off the Route de Casablanca, northeast of town; and the Amelkis Golf Club, 12km out on the Route de Ouarzazate (☎044 40 44 14, ℻044 40 44 15). All courses are open to non-members, with green fees at around 450dh per day.

Hammams A hammam is a Turkish-style steam bath (expect to pay around 10dh), with a succession of rooms from cool to hot, and endless supplies of hot and cold water, which you fetch in buckets. The usual procedure is to find a piece of floor space in the hot room, surround it with as many buckets of water as you feel you need, and lie in the heat to sweat out the dirt from your pores before scrubbing it off. A plastic bowl is useful for scooping the water from the buckets to wash with. You can also order a massage, in which you will be allowed to sweat, pulled about a bit to relax your muscles, and then rigorously scrubbed with a rough flannel glove (*kiis*). For many Moroccan women, the hammam is a social gathering place, in which women tourists are made very welcome too. Indeed, hammams turn out to be a highlight for many women travellers, and an excellent way to make contact with Moroccan women. There are quite a lot of hammams in the Medina; the three closest to, and all south of, the Jemaa el Fna are Hammam Polo on Rue de la Recette; Hammam Sidi Bouloukate on the same street as *Hôtel Afriquia*; and one at the northern end of Rue Riad Zitoun El Kadim. All three are open throughout the day, with separate entrances for men and women. North of the Jemaa el Fna, there's Hammam Dar el Bacha at 20 Rue Fatima

Zohra (daily: noon–7pm women only; at other times men only). Note that complete nudity is taboo, so you should keep your underwear on (bring a dry change) or wear a swimming costume, and change with a towel around you. In addition to these ordinary Moroccan hammams, an increasing number of upmarket hotels and riads now provide their own in-house hammam, where you can often book to bathe as a couple and not worry about the nudity thing; there are also upmarket tourist hammams such as Hammam Ziani on Rue Riad Zitoun el Jedid, open for both sexes (separate areas) daily 8am–10.30pm, and costing 50dh for a simple steam bath, or 270dh for an all-in package with massage and skin rub.

Laundry Most hotels offer a laundry service – in the cheapest places the chambermaid will usually do it herself. Failing that, try Pressing Oasis, 44 Rue Tarik Ibn Zaid, two doors from *Hotel Toulousain* in Guéliz, or Pressing du Sud, 10 Rue Bab Agnaou, near the Jemaa el Fna (entrance on Rue de la Recette) ☎044 42 91 12.

Newspapers The most reliable newsstand for American and British newspapers is outside the ONMT office on Av Mohammed V in Guéliz, though you'll find the *International Herald Tribune* and various British dailies on sale at stalls elsewhere, especially around the south side of Jemaa el Fna.

Pharmacies There are several along Av Mohammed V, including a good one, the Pharmacie de la Liberté, just off Pl de la Liberté. In the Medina, try Pharmacie de la Place and Pharmacie du Progrés on Rue Bab Agnaou just off the Jemaa el Fna. There's an all-night pharmacy (*depot de nuit*) by the Commissariat de Police on the Jemaa el Fna and another on Rue Khalid Ben Oualid near the fire station in Guéliz. Other late-opening and weekend outlets (*pharmacies de garde*) are listed in pharmacy windows and in local newspapers such as *Le Message de Marrakech*.

Swimming pools Many hotels (but, alas, not the *Mamounia*) allow non-residents to use their pools if you have a meal, or for a fee. Useful places to try are the *Grand Hotel Tazi* south of Jemaa el Fna and the *Hotel Yasmine* on Bd el Yarmouk, both charging 40–50dh per day.

Time Morocco is on Greenwich Mean Time all year, the same as Britain and Ireland in winter, an hour behind in summer. It's five hours ahead of the US east coast (EST) and eight ahead of the west coast (PST), an hour less in summer. It's also eight hours behind western Australia, ten hours behind eastern Australia, and twelve hours behind New Zealand (an hour more if daylight saving time is in operation in those places).

Tipping You're expected to tip waiters in cafés (1dh per person) and restaurants (5dh or so).

Trains Marrakesh's train station (☎090 20 30 40) is on Av Hassan II, on the edge of Guéliz. You can walk here from the centre of Guéliz in about fifteen minutes. Buses #3, #8, #10 and #14 run to the station from Pl Foucault by the Jemaa el Fna.

Vegetarian food Vegetarianism used to be pretty much unheard of in Morocco, but awareness is slowly increasing, especially in places used to dealing with tourists. Meat stock and animal fat are widely used in cooking, even in dishes that do not contain meat as such, and you may be best off just turning a blind eye to this. Some restaurants around the Jemaa el Fna that are popular with tourists do offer vegetarian versions of couscous and tajine. Otherwise, the cheaper restaurants serve omelettes, salads and sometimes *bisara* (pea soup), with fancier restaurants offering good salads and sometimes pizza. To tell people you're vegetarian, you could try *ana nabaati* in Arabic, or *je suis vegetarien/vegetarienne* in French. To reinforce the point, you could perhaps add *la akulu lehoum* (*wala hout*) in Arabic, or *je ne mange aucune sorte de viande* (*ni poisson*), both of which mean "I don't eat any kind of meat (or fish)".

Chronology

Chronology

1062–70 Marrakesh is founded by the Almoravids, a Berber religious fundamentalist movement from Mauritania led by Youssef Ben Tachfine, who makes the new city his capital.

1126–27 First city walls constructed.

1147 Marrakesh falls to the Almohads, another Berber religious movement, who destroy most of the Almoravid constructions, putting up new monuments in their place.

c.1150 Construction begins on the Koutoubia Mosque.

1184 Yacoub el Mansour takes the throne, heralding Marrrakesh's golden age. Poets and scholars arrive at court.

1269 Marrakesh falls to a new regime, the Merenids, with their capital at Fes. Marrakesh is relegated to second place among Morocco's cities.

1374–86 Merenid pretender Abdurrahman Ben Taflusin sets up a breakaway state in Marrakesh.

1521 Marrakesh is taken by a new Moroccan regime, the Saadians, who make it their capital.

1557 First burial at what is to become the Saadian Tombs.

1558 Mellah (Jewish quarter) established.

1578–1603 Under Ahmed el Mansour, the greatest Saadian sultan, Marrakesh sees a last burst of imperial splendour. El Badi Palace constructed.

1672 Alaouite sultan Moulay Ismail moves the capital to Meknes.

1750 Sidi Mohammed (later to become Sultan Mohammed III) is appointed governor of Marrakesh and embarks on a major restoration programme.

1792 The "mad sultan" Moulay Yazid becomes the last person to be buried in the Saadian Tombs.

1866–7 Bahia Palace built for Sultan Moulay Hassan's grand vizier Si Moussa.

1875 Encyclopaedia Britannica records how dilapidated the city has become.

1912 French "protectorate" established. Despite resistance led by local chieftain El Hiba, French forces occupy Marrakesh and begin construction of the Ville Nouvelle.

1918 T'hami el Glaoui appointed pasha of Marrakesh by the French colonialists.

1943 Moroccan Istiqlal (Independence) Party formed.

early 1950s Demands for independence increase, escalating into riots.

1956 Morocco becomes independent under Mohammed V, who re-establishes monarchical rule.

1967 Summer of Love. Hippies put Marrakesh on the overland trail.

1968 Crsoby, Stills and Nash record *Marrakesh Express* after taking the night train from Tangier.

1969 Jimi Hendrix visits Marrakesh and Essaouira.

1980s and 90s Migration from rural areas swells the city's population. Marrakesh re-establishes itself as Morocco's second biggest city after Casablanca.

1999 Mohammed VI becomes king.

2001 First Marrakesh Film Festival is held. Top prize is taken by Yamina Benguigui's *Inch'Allah Dimanche*.

2000s Huge rise in tourism, growth of riad industry, expansion of suburbs north and west of town.

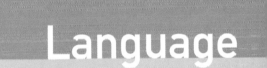

Language

Language

The most important language in Marrakesh is **Moroccan Arabic**, as different from the Arabic of the Middle East as Jamaican Patwa is from British or American English. For many Marrakshis, Arabic is in fact a second language, their first being **Tashelhait** (also called Chleuh), the indigenous Berber language spoken here since before the Arab invasion. Most people in Marrakesh also speak **French**, which is handy if you ever learned that at school.

Even if you learn no other Arabic phrases, it's useful to know the all-purpose greeting, *assalaam aleikum* ("peace to you"); the reply is *waaleikum salaam* ("and to you peace"). When speaking of anything in the future, Moroccans usually say *insha'allah* ("God willing"), and when talking of any kind of good fortune, they say *alhamdulillah* ("praise be to God"). It is normal to respond to these expressions by repeating them. Typically Moroccan phrases that you'll probably hear a lot include *makaynsh mooshkil* ("no problem") and *kif-kif* or *p'hal-p'hal* ("same thing", often meaning "I don't mind either" when someone needs to make a choice). If you really want to impress people, you could try some Tashelhait: "hello" is *manzakin* (with the stress on the second syllable) and "thank you" is *tanmeert*.

Useful terms and phrases

Here is some basic Arabic and French vocabulary for everyday communication. You may find it handy to supplement this list with a phrasebook, such as the *Rough Guide French Dictionary Phrasebook*.

Both Arabic and French have genders, even for inanimate objects, and the word ending varies slightly according to the gender. In the Arabic transliteration, we've used **kh** to represent the sound of ch in "loch", and **gh** to represent a gargling sound similar to a French "r". A **q** represents a "k" pronounced in the back of the throat rather than a "kw", and **j** is like the "zh" in Dr Zhivago; **r** should be trilled, as in Spanish. In Arabic words of more than one syllable, the stressed syllable is shown in bold.

English	**Arabic**	**French**
Basics and everyday phrases		
yes	**eyeh, naam**	oui
no	la	non
I	ena	moi
you (m/f)	**enta/entee**	vous
he	**hoo**wa	lui
she	**hee**ya	elle
we	**neh**noo	nous
they	hoom	ils/elles
(very) good	me**zyen** (**bzef**)	(très) bon
big	ke**beer**	grand
small	se**gheer**	petit
old	ke**deem**	vieux
new	je**deed**	nouveaux
a little	**shwee**ya	un peu
a lot	bzef	beaucoup
open	**mah**lul	ouvert
closed	mas**dud**	fermé
hello/how's it going?	le **bes**?	ça va?
good morning	sbah l'**kheer**	bonjour
good evening	msa l'**kheer**	bon soir
good night	**lei**la sa**ee**da	bonne nuit
goodbye	bise**la**ma	au revoir
who...?	shkoon...?	qui...?

English	Arabic	French
when...?	**im**ta...?	quand...?
why...?	a**lash**...?	pourquoi...?
how...?	ki**fesh**...?	comment...?
which/ what...?	**shnoo**...?	quel...?
is there...?	kayn...?	est-ce qu'il y a...?
do you have...?	**an**dak... /kayn...?	avez-vous...?
please	a**fak**/min **fad**lak	s'il vous plaît
	to a man or	
	a**fik**/min**fad**lik	
	to a woman	
thank you	**shuk**ran	merci
ok/agreed	**wak**ha	d'accord
that's enough/ that's all	**sa**fee	ça suffit
excuse me	is**mah**lee	excusez-moi
sorry/I'm very sorry	is**mah**lee/ ana **a**sif	pardon/je suis désolé
let's go	**nim**sheeyoo	on y va
go away	**im**shee	va t'en
I don't understand	mafa**hem**sh	je ne comprends pas
do you sepak english (m/f)	ta**ke**lem/ ta**kel**mna in**glee**si?	parlez-vous anglais?

where's...?	**fayn**...?	où est...?
the airport	el ma**tar**	l'aeroport
the train station	ma**hat**tat el tren	la gare de train
the bus station	ma**hat**tat el car	la gare routière
the bank	el bank	le banque
the hospital	el mo**stash**fa	le hôpital
near/far (from here)	qu**ray**ab/ba**eed** (min **hu**na)	près/loin (d'ici)
left	li**seer**	à gauche
right	li**meen**	à droit
straight ahead	**nee**shan	tout droit
here	**hi**na	ici
there	hi**nak**	là

hotel	**fun**duq	hôtel
do you have a room?	kayn beet?	avez-vous une chambre?
two beds	jooj **tlik**	deux lits
one big bed	**wa**had **tlik** ke**bir**	un grand lit
shower	**doosh**	douche
hot water	maa **skhoo**na	eau chaud
can I see?	**mum**kin a**shoof**ha?	je peux le voir?
key	sa**rut**	clé

I (don't) want...	**e**na (mish) b**gheet**...	je (ne) veux (pas)...
how much (money)?	sha**hal** (**flooss**)?	combien (d'argent)?
(that's) expensive	(**ha**da) gha**lee**	(c'est) cher

0	sifr	zéro
1	**wa**had	un
2	jooj	deux
3	**tla**ta	trois
4	ar**baa**	quatre
5	**kham**sa	cinq
6	**sit**ta	six
7	**se**baa	sept
8	te**man**ya	huit
9	**ti**saoud	neuf
10	**ash**ra	dix
11	ha**dash**ar	onze
12	et**nash**ar	douze
13	tala**tash**ar	treize
14	arba**tash**ar	quatorze
15	khams**tash**ar	quinze
16	sit**tash**ar	seize
17	seba**tash**ar	dix-sept
18	taman**tash**ar	dix-huit
19	tisa**tash**ar	dix-neuf
20	ash**reen**	vingt
21	**wa**had wa ash**reen**	vingt-et-un
22	jooj wa ash**reen**	vingt-deux
30	tala**teen**	trente
40	arba**een**	quarante
50	kham**seen**	cinqante
60	sit**teen**	soixante
70	saba**een**	soixante-dix
80	taman**een**	quatre vingts
90	tisa**een**	quatre-vingt-dix
100	mia	cent
121	mia wa **wa**had wa ash**reen**	cent vingt-et-un

English	Arabic	French
200	mia**teen**	deux cents
300	**tolta** mia	trois cents
1000	alf	mille
a half	nuss	demi
a quarter	**rob**a	quart

Days and times

Monday	nahar el it **neen**	lundi
Tuesday	nahar et telat	mardi
Wednesday	nahar el **arbaa**	mercredi
Thursday	nahar el khe**mis**	jeudi
Friday	nahar el jemaa	vendredi
Saturday	nahar es sabt	samedi
Sunday	nahar el had	dimanche
yesterday	im**ba**rih	hier
today	el yoom	aujourd'hui
tomorrow	**ghe**da	demain
what time is it?	sha**hal** fisa'a?	quelle heure est-il?
one o'clock	sa'a **wah**da	une heure
2.15	jooj wa **rob**a	deux heures et quart
3.30	tlata wa nuss	trois heures et demi
4.45	arbaa ila **rob**a	quatre heures moins quart

Food and drink basics

restaurant	**mat**aam	restaurant
breakfast	if**tar**	petit déjeuner
egg	beyd	ouef
butter	**zib**da	beurre
jam	marma**lad**	confiture
cheese	**jib**na	fromage
yoghurt	**ray**eb	yaourt
salad	sa**la**ta	salade
olives	zi**toun**	olives
bread	khobz	pain
salt	**mel**ha	sel
pepper (without)	ha**roor** (bi**lesh**)	piment (sans)
sugar	**suk**kar	sucre
the bill	el hi**sab**	l'addition
fork	for**shaat**	fourchette
knife	**moo**sa	couteau
spoon	**miel**aqa	cuillère
plate	tab**seel**	assiette

Meat, poultry and fish

meat	**lah**em	viande
beef	**baq**ri	boeuf
chicken	djaj	poulet
lamb	**hou**li	mouton
liver	**kib**da	foie
pigeon	**ham**am	pigeon
fish	hout	poisson
prawns	**qam**bri	crevettes

Vegetables

vegetables	khadra**wat**	légumes
artichoke	qoq	artichaut
aubergine	badin**jan**	aubergine
beans	**loo**bia	haricots
onions	**bas**al	oignons
potatoes	ba**ta**ta	patates
tomatoes	ma**tee**sha	tomates

Fruits and nuts

almonds	looz	amandes
apple	tu**fah**	pomme
banana	ba**nan**	banane
dates	tmer	dattes
figs	ker**mooss**	figues
grapes	**ai**nab	raisins
lemon	li**moon**	limon
melon	bat**tikh**	melon
orange	li**moon**	orange
pomegranate	**roo**man	granade
prickly pear (cactus fruit)	hen**diya**	figues de Barbarie
strawberry	**frow**la	fraise
watermelon	del**lah**	pastèque

Beverages

water	maa	de l'eau
mineral water	Sidi Ali/Sidi Harazem (brand names)	eau minérale
ice	je**lee**di	glace
ice cream	glace	glace
milk	ha**leeb**	lait
coffee	**qah**wa	café
coffee with a little milk	nuss nuss	café cassé
coffee with plenty of milk	**qah**wa bi ha**leeb**	café au lait/ café crème
tea (with mint/ wormwood)	**a**tay (bi **na**na /**shee**ba)	thé (à la menthe/ à l'absinthe)
juice	a**seer**	jus

LANGUAGE Useful terms and phrases

Useful terms and phrases

English	Arabic	French
beer	**bir**ra	bière
wine	sha**rab**	vin
almond milk	a**seer** looz	jus d'amande
apple milkshake	a**seer** tu**fah**	jus de pomme
banana milkshake	a**seer** ba**nan**	jus des bananes
orange juice	a**seer** li**moon**	jus d'orange
mixed fruit milkshake	-	jus panache

Common dishes and foods

bisara	thick pea soup, usually served with olive oil and cumin
chakchouka	a vegetable stew not unlike ratatouille, though sometimes containing meat or eggs
couscous aux sept legumes	seven-vegetable couscous (sometimes vegetarian, though often made with meat stock)
harira	bean soup, usually also containing pasta and meat
kefta	minced meat (usually lamb)
loobia	bean stew
mechoui	roast lamb
merguez	small, spicy dark red sausages – typically lamb, though sometimes of beef – usually grilled over charcoal

pastilla	sweet pigeon or chicken pie with cinnamon and filo pastry; a speciality of Fes
(pommes) frites	French fries
salade Marocaine	salad of tomato and cucumber, finely chopped
tajine	a Moroccan casserole cooked over charcoal in a thick ceramic bowl (which is what the word really refers to) with a conical lid
tajine aux olives et citron	tajine of chicken with olive and preserved lemon
tanjia	a Marrakshi speciality, jugged beef – the term in fact refers to the jug

Breads and pastries

briouats/ doits de Fatima	sweet filo pastry with a savoury filling, a bit like a miniature pastilla
briouats au miel	sweet filo pastry envelopes filled with nuts and honey
cornes de gazelles (Fr.)/ kab l-ghazl (Ar.)	marzipan-filled, banana-shaped pastry horns
harsha	flat, leavened griddle bread with a gritty crust, served at cafés for breakast
millefeuille	custard slice
msammen	flat griddle bread made from dough sprinkled with oil, rolled out and folded over several times, rather like an Indian paratha

Glossary

Alaouites (also spelt **Alawites**) The dynasty to which Morocco's present king, Mohammed VI, belongs, and which first came to power in 1668. The Alaouites trace their ancestry back to the Prophet Mohammed.

Almohads A religious movement of Berbers based at Tinmal in the Atlas. They took Marrakesh in 1147 and made it the capital of an empire stretching from Spain to Tunisia.

Almoravids A fundamentalist movement of Mauritanian Berber nomads who conquered Marrakesh in 1062 and held it until 1147.

argan A tree that grows only in the south of Morocco, bearing a fruit whose pip yields a sweet and much prized oil.

bab Gate or door.

ben Son of, eg "Ben Youssef" meaning "the son of Youssef".

Berbers The indigenous population of Morocco prior to the seventh-century Arab invasion. Even today, Marrakesh is as much a Berber city as an Arab one, and the regional Berber language, Tashelhait, is widely spoken.

calèche Horse-drawn carriage.

dar Mansion or palace.

derb Alley.

Fes (also spelt **Fez** in English, **Fès** in French) Marrakesh's long-time rival as Morocco's cultural and political capital, and still considered its main spiritual, musical and culinary centre.

fondouk Caravanserai; an old inn for travelling merchants.

ginbri Skin covered two- or three-string lutes, originally from West Africa, and a favourite Gnaoua instrument.

Gnaoua Member of a Sufi (Muslim mystic) fraternity of musicians, originally from West Africa (the word *gnaoua* comes from the same root as Guinea).

hammam In principle just a bath or bathroom, but it refers in particular to a traditional steam bath with a hotroom, much the same as a Turkish bath.

jellaba A long garment with sleeves and a hood.

kasbah A fortified area within a city, often the citadel. In the case of Marrakesh,

it's a walled residential district in the southwest of the Medina.

kissaria Covered market, especially the textile market at the heart of the Medina's souks.

koubba A dome, but also used for the domed building constructed over the tomb of a saint.

marabout Itinerant holy man or woman, often credited with divine powers (to exorcize demons, for example).

medersa Religious school where pupils are taught to read and write, and study the Koran.

Merenids A Berber dynasty from eastern Morocco who took power in Fes in 1248, conquered Marrakesh in 1269, and remained in power until 1465.

mihrab The niche in a mosque indicating the direction of Mecca, and thus of prayer.

minbar The wooden pulpit in a mosque.

minzah A pavilion in a park.

moulay A descendant of the Prophet Mohammed.

moussem Annual local festival celebrating a saint's day.

oued Wadi; a seasonal watercourse.

pisé Clay and straw used for construction of walls and buildings.

raï Originally from Algeria, this is the most popular type of pop music in Morocco, mainly in the form of love songs.

riad A patio garden and, by extension, a house with a patio garden.

Saadians A dynasty of descendants of the Prophet, from the Souss Valley in Morocco's far south. They took Marrakesh in 1521, made it their capital, and ruled until 1668.

sidi Respectful term used to address a man; also used to refer to a Muslim saint.

souk Market, in particular a part of the Medina where shops or workshops of one type are gathered.

Sufi Muslim mystic, belonging to a brotherhood (there are several brotherhoods in Morocco).

thuya (also spelt **thuja**; **arar** in Arabic) An aromatic mahogany-like hardwood from a local coniferous tree.

Yacoub el Mansour The third Almohad sultan (ruled 1184–99), whose reign arguably marked Marrakesh's golden age.

Youssef Ben Tachfine Marrakesh's founder, the first Almoravid sultan, buried to the south of the Koutoubia Mosque.

zaouia The sanctuary established around the tomb of a marabout, often the base of a Sufi (mystic) religious brotherhood.

zellij Tilework, especially a form in which small pieces of ceramic tiles are cut into shapes that fit into a geometrical mosaic design, usually based on a star with a specific number of points.

Morocco

Made to Measure

small print & Index

SMALL PRINT

A Rough Guide to Rough Guides

In 1981, Mark Ellingham, a recent graduate in English from Bristol University, was travelling in Greece on a tiny budget and couldn't find the right guidebook. With a group of friends he wrote his own guide, combining a contemporary, journalistic style with a practical approach to travellers' needs. That first Rough Guide was a student scheme that became a publishing phenomenon. Today, Rough Guides include recommendations from shoestring to luxury and cover hundreds of destinations around the globe, including almost every country in the Americas and Europe, more than half of Africa and most of Asia and Australasia. Millions of readers relish Rough Guides' wit and inquisitiveness as much as their enthusiastic, critical approach and value-for-money ethos. The guides' ever-growing team of authors and photographers is spread all over the world.

In the early 1990s, Rough Guides branched out of travel, with the publication of Rough Guides to World Music, Classical Music and the Internet. All three have become benchmark titles in their fields, spearheading the publication of a range of more than 350 titles under the Rough Guide name, including phrasebooks, waterproof maps, music guides from Opera to Heavy Metal, reference works as diverse as Conspiracy Theories and Shakespeare, and popular culture books from iPods to Poker. Rough Guides also produce a series of more than 120 World Music CDs in partnership with World Music Network.

Visit www.roughguides.com to see our latest publications.

Rough Guide travel images are available for commercial licensing at www.roughguidespictures.com

Publishing information

This second edition published April 2007 by Rough Guides Ltd, 80 Strand, London WC2R 0RL; 345 Hudson St, 4th Floor, New York, NY 10014, USA.

Distributed by the Penguin Group
Penguin Books Ltd, 80 Strand, London WC2R 0RL
Penguin Group (USA), 375 Hudson St, NY 10014, USA
14 Local Shopping Centre, Panchsheel Park, New Delhi 110017, India
Penguin Group (Australia), 250 Camberwell Rd, Camberwell, Victoria 3124, Australia
Penguin Group (Canada), 10 Alcorn Ave, Toronto, ON M4V 1E4, Canada
Penguin Group (NZ), 67 Apollo Drive, Mairangi Bay, Auckland 1310, New Zealand
Typeset in Bembo and Helvetica to an original design by Henry Iles.
Cover concept by Peter Dyer.

Printed and bound in China
© Daniel Jacobs, April 2007

No part of this book may be reproduced in any form without permission from the publisher except for the quotation of brief passages in reviews.
164pp includes index

A catalogue record for this book is available from the British Library

ISBN 10: 1-84353-762-1

ISBN 13: 9-781-84353-762-5

1 3 5 7 9 8 6 4 2

Help us update

We've gone to a lot of effort to ensure that the second edition of Marrakesh DIRECTIONS is accurate and up-to-date. However, things change – places get "discovered", opening hours are notoriously fickle, restaurants and rooms raise prices or lower standards. If you feel we've got it wrong or left something out, we'd like to know, and if you can remember the address, the price, the phone number, so much the better.

We'll credit all contributions, and send a copy of the next edition (or any other DIRECTIONS guide or Rough Guide if you prefer) for the best letters. Everyone who writes to us and isn't already a subscriber will receive a copy of our full-colour thrice-yearly newsletter. Please mark letters: "Marrakesh DIRECTIONS Update" and send to: Rough Guides, 80 Strand, London WC2R 0RL, or Rough Guides, 4th Floor, 345 Hudson St, New York, NY 10014. Or send an email to mail@roughguides.com

Have your questions answered and tell others about your trip at www.roughguides.atinfopop.com

Rough Guide credits

Text editor: Sarah Eno
Layout: Ajay Verma
Photography: Suzanne Porter & Dan Eitzen
Cartography: Karobi Gogoi

Picture editor: Simon Bracken & Nicole Newman
Proofreader: Helen Castell
Production: Aimee Hampson
Cover design: Chlöe Roberts

The author

Daniel Jacobs is a major-league Moroccophile who has contributed to numerous Rough Guides including Morocco, Egypt, India, West Africa and Mexico titles. He is also the author of the *Rough Guide to Israel and the Palestinian Territories*, and co-author of the *Rough Guide to Tunisia*. He lives in South London.

Readers' letters

Thanks to all those readers of the first edition who took the trouble to write in with their amendments and additions. Apologies for any misspellings or omissions.

Jim and Margie Campbell, Paul Trusker

Photo credits

All images © Rough Guides except the following:

Front image: Koutoubia Minaret © Alamy
Back image: Djemaa al Fna © Ian Cumming/Axiom
p.5 Riyad Al Moussika – Dassin andalous © Riyâd Al Moussika
p.9 Pacha Disco © Pacha
p.13 Jardin Majorelle © Eye Ubiquitous/CORBIS
p.13 Saadian Tomb © Hamish Brown
p.20 Cooking school at the Maison Arabe © Maison Arabe
p.23 Saadian Tombs Marrakesh © Gary Cook/Alamy
p.24 Courtyard at the theological school of Ali ben Youssef © Martin Harvey / Alamy
p.27 Islamic Arts Museum © Daniel Jacobs
p.28 Marrakesh child having henna tattoo © Tim Mossford/Alamy
p.29 Hammam © Maison Arabe
p.29 Maison Arabe – Kasbah by night © Maison Arabe
p.29 Oliveri ice-cream © Daniel Jacobs
p.32 Opening party, Marrakesh International Film Festival 2005 © S.Cardinale/People Avenue/Corbis
p.32 Celebrity chef at Casa Lalla © Casa Lalla
p.33 Sean Connery – 2004 Marrakesh International Film Festival ©Jean Blondin/Reuters/Corbis
p.34 Musician Jemaa El Fna © Joanne Moyes/Alamy

p.35 Food Stall in Jemaa el-Fna Square © Sandro Vannini/Corbis
p.39 Marrakech garden and artist studio ©Bernard Grilly/Museart/Corbis
p.40 Pacha © Pacha
p.41 Diamant Noir ©Diamant Noir
p.41 Paradise © Paradise
p.45 Golf © Mococcan National Tourist Office
p.46 Marathon © The Marrakesh Marathon
p.46 Moussem © Sylvain Grandadam/Robert Harding
p.47 Morocco Koutoubia mosque © David Kilpatrick/Alamy
p.47 Gnaoua festival © Gnaoua
p.47 Marrakesh Festival © The Marrakesh Festival
p.66 La Mamounia waiters © La Mamounia
p.74 Souq in Marrakesh © Simon Bracken
p.94 Pacha © Pacha
p.95 Paradise Disco © Paradise
p.96 Chesterfields terrasse piscine © Chesterfields
p.97 Diamant Noir © Diamant Noir
p.98 Pacha © Pacha
p.115 Casa Lalla © Casa Lalla
p.119 Maison Arabe yassmina © Maison Arabe
p.124 Riyad Al Moussika – Chambre Al Azrak © Riyad Al Moussika

Index

Maps are marked in colour

INDEX